WHAT KIND OF

WORLD

DO YOU WANT?

Here's How We Can Get It

Jim Lord

with Pam McAllister

PRE-PUBLICATION
HONORARY GIFT EDITION

This book is available to be purchased in quantity by
institutions and individuals who wish to use it as a gift.
Customized editions are also available.

For more information about giving this book to honor
those who have contributed to society, please send an
email to gifts@whatkindofworld.com.

The authors are grateful for permission to include the following previously copyrighted
material: Excerpt from "Tearing Down That Wall" by Peter Robinson; first published in
The Weekly Standard, June 23, 1997; reprinted by permission of the publisher. Excerpt
from "Mountain Music" © 1997 by Scott Russell Sanders; first published in *Orion* (Winter
1997); reprinted by permission of the author.

Printed in the United States of America

Imagine if all the people

who want to change the world

knew they could.

I am convinced that far more
idealistic aspiration exists than is
ever evident. Just as the rivers we
see are much less numerous than
the underground streams, so the
idealism that is visible is minor
compared to what men and women
carry in their hearts, unreleased
or scarcely released. Mankind is
waiting and longing for those who
can accomplish the task of untying
what is knotted and bringing the
underground waters to the surface.

—Albert Schweitzer

PLEASE WRITE IN THE MARGINS

Everything in this book is offered to stimulate your thinking.

As you turn the pages of this slim volume, allow your experience to be foremost. Write your insights in the book.

Really.

Most of us hear the grade-school librarian in the back of our heads and treat a book like a sacred object. To that I say: Go ahead, write in it. Make friends with it. Make it yours.

Contents

WHAT KIND OF

WORLD

DO YOU WANT?

WHAT IS THIS WORLD COMING TO?

The book you hold in your hands was born from a keen sense of urgency about the state of society and the future of our planet.

For most people, those words conjure up worrisome images of war, poverty, environmental degradation. A shared sense of looming disaster is fueled by constant attention to the heartbreak of September 11, the devastation of tsunamis and hurricanes, and countless other calamities actual and feared.

Many people believe that civilization is descending to new depths and the very existence of life on Earth is at risk. With good reason. We can find ample evidence that we're making a mess of things.

Against such a backdrop, how can anyone honestly believe the future might turn out well?

My sense of urgency springs from an entirely different source. Surprising as it may sound, I believe humanity is poised to ascend to new heights—and indeed has already begun to do so, in ways often invisible to our view. As you page through this book, I think you'll find plenty of evidence to support this unusual claim.

The world I see is vibrant, vital, and filled with promise. When I take a good hard look at this reality, I experience a new kind of urgency, founded on confidence and hope. Of course, you will decide whether to buy this premise.

ONE

WHERE DO WE STAND?

WE HAVE SO MUCH
GOING FOR US

Two of us are at the front of a small meeting room, unrolling a sheet of plain white paper, 20 feet long, and taping it to the wall. In a few minutes, a group of people will arrive to begin a workshop.

Soon we'll be asking them:

> What do you see in the world, what do you see
> in your world, that gives you confidence in the
> future?

The first time I asked this question, a little more than a decade ago, I was afraid I'd be up there in front of a silent room. And indeed, the question has proven to be surprisingly challenging to answer. For most people, it seems to come out of the blue.

When I ask the question of this group, they hesitate before speaking. After a few moments, I hear a tentative voice. "How about women? The ascent of women into positions of power?" I write these words in the middle of the paper on the wall.

Another pause before the next idea is offered. I write it up: "advances in medicine." Someone else observes that there seems to be renewed interest in the spiritual dimension of life.

Then someone says, "the invention of the Internet."

"Wait a minute," another interrupts. "The Internet is creating some big problems. Sure, it lets us communicate with people far away, but we spend way too much time in front of our computers and not enough time in the real world. What about the damage it's doing?"

I've heard this question before. I know it's likely to be in the back of everyone's mind: "Isn't there a downside to every upside?"

"If you look for it, you can find something wrong with just about anything," I suggest. "Right now, we're trying something different: intentionally focusing on finding things of value. That's what can fuel the future. So let's experiment and suspend our ability to discern the downside, just for the moment." (We'll soon see why this choice is so crucial.)

And I write "the invention of the Internet" on the wall.

As often happens, addressing the what-about-the-downside question unleashes the group's creativity. Someone expands on the Internet, observing that communications technology has enhanced freedom of speech. The earlier remark about the ascent of women prompts a comment about "more acceptance of human diversity." The pace picks up as one person's idea sparks another's.

The paper begins to fill and an astonishing range of assets and forces is revealed.

> Increased awareness of the importance of the natural environment.
>
> The spread of ideals such as democracy and universal public education.
>
> Widespread voluntarism.
>
> The commitment people make to care for children.
>
> Our ability to laugh.

I can feel the energy in the room rise as we begin to see a different world than the one portrayed on the evening news. A different world than we often talk about in casual conversations at home, at work, even at the kids' softball game, when so often the talk gravitates to what's wrong and how bad things are.

At the end of the day, I stay after the group has left, looking at the work we've put on the wall. I'm moved by how we've begun to develop our collective ability to see all we have going for us—the tailwinds the world offers.

And I wonder why those tailwinds are often out of our view. Why does the question I asked the group seem so unusual?

THE "WOE ARE WE" CONVERSATION

A few years ago I was having lunch by myself in a restaurant. At the table next to me a couple of young men were talking (all right, they were grumbling) about their work. Behind me the same kind of conversation was going on. It dawned on me that these folks had tacitly agreed that this was the way they would talk to each other.

It was what I've come to call the "woe are we" conversation.

It's an interesting social convention: We often connect with each other by talking about what's wrong, what we don't want, how awful things are. This habitual pattern of conversation is as comfortable as an old pair of shoes. We could just as easily talk about what we want, and what we have going for us that will get us there. But it's not the socially accepted thing to do.

Those simple habits of thought and talk create a culture.

I'd go so far as to propose that we've created a social agreement—a silent, unexamined assumption—that we must talk about problems and limitations because they are what's *real*. Although this belief usually remains unspoken, it shapes our thoughts and dominates our language: In American slang, "let's get real," often means "let's talk about what's wrong." Often implied is how helpless we are to change anything.

The strength of this convention was brought home to me recently when a gentleman reputed to be the most powerful in Bermuda hosted a working lunch for people involved in social sector causes in that island nation. The gathering was carefully designed to draw attention to tailwinds and assets, especially those that support people in contributing to society and making a difference with their lives.

As the meeting drew to a close, I stood in front of the group for a question and answer session. The first question came from one of the former premiers of the country.

"How long have you been here, Jim? Have you read the local paper?"

A couple more questions revealed what was behind his polite query. He wanted me to acknowledge the downside of paradise. He wanted to make sure we didn't sweep the issues under the carpet.

I certainly was aware of this account of life on the island. But as far as I'm concerned, asking "What about the problems?" is beside the point. It's simply a routine, a habit (you might call it the default setting we return to time and again), even for people like this gentleman who are known for their "can-do" attitude.

(A woman sitting next to the former premier reminded him of how often he takes a different stance. "I know you," she said. "And for heaven's sake, you count the number of times in a day that you say 'yes.'")

We can follow the norm and investigate thoroughly the phenomena that we call problems, if we want to do that. We can also spend time on debates about whether it's "fair" or "truthful" to focus on assets instead of taking a so-called impartial view of the world.

I prefer to take a more practical approach and leave such philosophizing to others. The way I see it, we have a strategic decision to make: Based on everything we know about human beings, what is the *best* fuel for the bold, sustained action that will realize potentials?

Do we get farther if we focus on problems or if we pay attention to assets? As you'll see, there are good reasons to bet on the latter.

WHY IS IT THAT WE'RE
SO OCCUPIED WITH PROBLEMS?

One sunny Sunday morning several years ago, I flew into Perth, Western Australia. It was a working trip, so I had with me several suitcases, including a 70-pound trunk filled with books and papers.

At the airport taxi stand, I started to apologize to the driver for burdening him with such a quantity of luggage. A huge smile on his face, he scooped up my heavy cases and deftly hoisted the trunk onto the roof of his cab.

Delighted with the sunshine and his friendly, upbeat demeanor, I thought I'd found utopia. On the ride into town, catching a glimpse of Perth's famous black swans on the river, I asked my new friend what he liked most about living in Perth.

"Well, it's not as bad as a lot of other places."

"How's that?" I asked, more than a little baffled by his response.

"There isn't as much crime. There isn't as much pollution. There isn't as much poverty. It's not as bad as a lot of other places. Yeah, that's what I like best about living here."

Well, I suppose that's one way of looking at it.

Even today, I still find it curious that problems are so central to our awareness.

It seems to begin very early in our lives. Researchers put small tape recorders on the backs of 5-year-olds. They found that today's children are growing up in homes where as much as 90 percent of the conversation is about how bad things are, what was done wrong, who is to blame, and what not to do.

As we become adults, the deficit mindset is reinforced as we are swept into the intellectual climate of critique that has expanded in the last several decades. We are taught valuable lessons in how to be critical and analytical, to deconstruct, expose, debunk.

This worldview is fortified by deep and pervasive cultural and intellectual traditions.

The idea of original sin, according to defrocked priest Matthew Fox, has dominated Western culture for more than a thousand years, providing a foundational belief for many. (It wasn't always so. Fox tells us that creation itself—the original blessing—was at the heart of Christianity until St. Augustine in the fourth century.) A friend who is a devout Catholic has told me of the prayer before communion that begins "Lord, I am not worthy" (words he has boldly replaced with "Lord, I am worthy, for I was made in Your image").

Today, such long-held beliefs have been supplemented by modern social science, which has provided a generous supply of new models of human deficit.

Here's one example: In the space of just a few decades, professional diagnostic terms—depression, attention deficit disorder, codependency, addiction—have spread widely in popular culture. This language, and the disease-oriented framework it reflects, have come to dominate how we think and talk about our inner lives. We may even have learned how to be mentally ill.

With all of this energy devoted to a deficit-oriented worldview, is it any wonder so many of us grow up believing that problems are at the center of our lives? Or even that people don't *have* problems, they *are* problems, and that life itself is a problem to be solved?

Our attention to problems is understandable. It may be that we're born with our brains hard-wired that way. After all, our ancestors had to be acutely aware of danger in order to survive.

On top of any innate tendencies, we also wire our brains through our daily actions. We human beings are intensely social creatures. We learn by watching and copying what other people do. Researchers who study how our brains work are finding that this learning happens through the operation of special brain cells called mirror neurons. These cells perform a most amazing function: When you sit perfectly still and watch someone else do something, your mirror neurons fire exactly as if you were doing the action yourself. You can literally feel what the other person is going through.

This astonishing discovery starts to explain why we tend to take on the feelings, language, and beliefs of those around us—why we follow along when our lunch companions complain about how bad things are. The study of mirror neurons is beginning to provide a biological understanding of empathy, human connection, learning, and even the transmission of culture.

There's more. A constantly repeated behavior creates and reinforces pathways in the basal ganglia, the part of the brain where habits live. When we habitually focus on problems, we may actually change our own brains in ways that make it more likely we'll continue to pay attention to problems.

With all this going on inside our brains, it starts to sound like it might be a large task to rewire ourselves in another direction. The encouraging news, it seems to me, is that it is possible. After all, if we've learned our problem-oriented culture by imitating other people, we can learn (and teach) new behaviors in the same way. And new habits can replace old ones.

But it's reasonable to ask at the outset: *Why make the effort?*

After all, there is a certain liberation in being critical and cutting right to the problem. And better to be a staunch social critic than a feeble apologist for an unjust status quo—if we see those as the only available options.

Yet as we'll see, we pay a high price when we let criticism become the dominant way we look at the world. I believe it is time to reconsider the utility of the deficit-based stance, just as we've worked to rise above other aspects of human behavior that have outlived their usefulness.

CLOSET IDEALISM

Beneath the critical veneer of modern life lies a deep hidden reservoir of idealism.

Every time we criticize the way things are, we indirectly signal our desire for a better world. Every statement about what's wrong is actually an unarticulated hope. Every social critic wants the world to be a better place.

Yet it takes courage to depart from the standard conversations of complaint.

"To be gloomy is to be serious," writes William Safire. "to be joyful is seen as frivolous or deceptive."

My colleague and friend Anne Nickerson echoes this insight. Anne heads a family foundation in Sheridan, Wyoming, a dynamic community of 15,000 people. She says she used to feel timid about expressing her aspirations in meetings with others in the community.

"I didn't want to look silly," she admits. "Sometimes people can make you feel that way."

After organizing a community-wide dialogue that used the principles in this book, Anne realized how many people had the same high hopes for the community as she did. She vowed to speak up with confidence, instead of holding back on her thoughts and ideas. As a pathway, the people who Anne had gathered created a Center for Vital Community, a permanent, daily convening point for conversations of consequence and action.

Anne's sense that others share her high aspirations for society is supported by the research of Paul Ray, who has described an emerging worldview held by a growing segment of the population that he calls "cultural creatives." These people share values that range from personal authenticity to ecological sustainability. They're optimistic and altruistic. They're looking for more meaningful lives and working to create a better future.

Ray believes that the more than 50 million cultural creatives in the United States, and nearly 100 million in the European Union, have already begun to create a new culture. And yet they are largely invisible, even to one another. Each individual thinks they're alone in their beliefs. At most, they know a few friends who share their views.

They don't talk about their values in public because they feel out of step with social norms. Like Anne, they don't want to be embarrassed or put down. So they remain unaware of their numbers and their potential power.

For Americans who came of age during the social upheavals of the 1960s and 70s, this new culture may simply represent a return to their roots. A few years ago, I facilitated a board retreat for an organization that wanted to elevate its contribution to society. At the beginning of our time together, a board member questioned the idealism inherent in the approach I was suggesting.

I made a point of sitting with him at lunch, and learned that he had served in the Peace Corps as a young man. So often, the flame of idealism and activism that burned so brightly in youth is waiting for the embers, still faintly glowing, to be fanned back to life.

By the end of the day, and without my ever answering his objections, he said to the group, "I began the day as the greatest skeptic of these ideas. I end it as the greatest champion of them." Sometimes a bit of reflection is all it takes to remind ourselves of our deepest beliefs.

It's time to acknowledge how many others share our hopes and dreams. Heaven forbid, they might even be closet idealists.

TWO

DO WE *CHOOSE*
THE FUTURE?

THE CHOICE TO SEE
HIDDEN STRENGTHS

On a cold, windy November day, Doug Collins flings open the door of a classroom at Harrow School in London. Doug, a member of the school's leadership team, waves me inside the dimly-lit room. It's lined with long rows of empty benches without backs. "Here's where Winston Churchill was a somewhat grudging student," Doug tells me. "In fact, he'd been placed in what today would be called the remedial reading class."

Doug knows I'll be interested in Churchill's early years at the school. From this austere room and unpromising beginning, Churchill went on to become a world leader — one who could see a future that marked him as "unrealistic" at best, a madman at worst.

Consider how Churchill appealed to the beleaguered British people in the grim days of the summer of 1940. The Nazi war machine had overrun Europe. The Battle of France had been lost, a debacle in which more than 30,000 British soldiers had died. The British, their empire in decline and their confidence destroyed by the carnage of World War I, stood alone against the threat of imminent invasion. Bombs fell in the heart of London. Frightened people huddled in the subways.

In the face of such a fearful reality, Churchill boldly declared that he was taking office with "buoyancy and hope." He called the British people forward to victory in what he knew would be "their finest hour." As Churchill's biographer, Isaiah Berlin, wrote, "He created a heroic mood and turned the fortunes of the Battle of Britain not by catching the mood of his surroundings but by being impervious to it, as he had been to so many of the passing shades and tones."

Churchill saw and revealed the fundamental strength of his country and its people, a strength that had been hidden by fear and despair. Seeing this inherent worth made it possible for him to hold a hopeful image of the future, even in Britain's darkest moment, and to inspire others to share that vision.

I tell this story often. For me, it is an especially moving reminder that we can choose how we hold the past, present, and future. Churchill exercised this kind of choice when he discerned the path to victory in the darkness of defeat.

I'm also encouraged when I realize that the choices Churchill made were not easy for him as a human being. After all, he experienced a great deal of what today we'd call depression, and often felt he stood alone in his beliefs.

Many of us have had the Churchillian experience of seeing strengths where others see limitations, even if in smaller ways, even if only for a fleeting moment. Each of us manages, at times, to transcend the pervasive background music of our culture: the dominant chorus of cynicism, irony, and hopelessness.

Each of us sees, from time to time, the fundamental value and strength in those around us (and sometimes even in ourselves).

BUT MUST WE
"FACE REALITY"?

In everyday life, most of us are held back by our sense that our resources are limited and that circumstances control our destiny.

Even if we are successful by society's standards, we restrict our options and behave as if necessity, reasonableness, feasibility, and "the givens" act as natural law, ruling our daily lives.

The conventional assumption that we must "face reality" is without a doubt the greatest single constraint on human imagination, vision, and enterprise. It is an arbitrary, self-imposed limit on our beliefs, especially our belief in what is possible.

What happens when we choose a different place to stand? What happens when we intentionally *select* the aspects of reality that we want to use as our foundation?

Left blind and deaf by an early childhood illness, Helen Keller said, "So much has been given to me, I have not time to ponder over that which has been denied."

Across the globe in a remote village in Nepal, a grandmother hears that reading and writing classes will be offered in a nearby village. She invests all she has, the equivalent of 12 cents U.S. The program also allows her to be part of a group that rents a loom and starts a weaving business. Two years later, the "poor widow" sees herself as a wealthy woman, so much that she gives money to a sick relative.

"How good it feels that I have so much I can share," she says.

Most of us would be inclined to consider her impover-
ished, rather than the wealthy woman she knows herself
to be. And we might focus on what she, like Helen Keller,
had been denied, rather than on the gifts she saw she pos-
sessed.

Where we choose to stand shapes what we see as possible.

This idea is a first step toward opening the way for
us to do the incredible. Whether we want to influence a
country, as Churchill did, or an individual—or even ourselves—the key is how we look at the world, rather than
the way the world *is*.

What might become possible if we chose to have more
"unrealistic" moments, if we multiplied them and let them
become a larger part of how we meet the world?

No matter how daunting the deficits, we can choose
how we will experience life.

> We who lived in concentration camps
> can remember the men who walked
> through the huts comforting others,
> giving away their last piece of bread.
> They may have been few in number,
> but they offer sufficient proof that
> everything can be taken away from
> a man but one thing: the last of the
> human freedoms, to choose one's atti-
> tude in any given set of circumstances,
> to choose one's own way.
>
> —Viktor Frankl

THE IMPOSSIBLE
HAS BECOME POSSIBLE

Again and again, people have made choices that eluded others and the impossible has become possible. A human footprint on the moon, the fall of the Berlin wall, the end of apartheid, a computer on every desk, living with another person's heart beating in one's chest.

We're defining, all the time, what's possible for society, how high our aspirations are, and what we believe is desirable and good. As a result, even ideals once dismissed as "utopian" are now widely shared: parliamentary democracy, universal suffrage, freedom of speech and religion, public education, full employment and social security, rights for women and minorities.

Perhaps most astonishing, in recent years we have taken responsibility for the entire Earth and all living things. Like so many of the greatest advances, that one has crept up on us so slowly that we're hardly aware of it.

Likewise, we rarely pause to notice that human cooperation on a global scale, once considered an idealistic fantasy, has become a reality.

The eradication of smallpox, just a few decades ago, marked the very first time people organized at the global level and accomplished the seemingly impossible. At one time, smallpox was so widespread that most experts believed it couldn't be controlled. (Indeed, more people died from smallpox in the last century than died in all of its wars.)

The successful effort was founded on a bold, even extreme idea: to completely eliminate the disease from the face of the Earth. The director of the campaign, Dr. D.A. Henderson, was called naïve and utopian for taking that stand, yet that very boldness was crucial to the success of the whole endeavor.

The campaign against smallpox appears to have been brief: The World Health Organization launched the effort in 1967 and declared the job complete in 1980. The real story is how long it actually took to come about. Smallpox thrived for nearly two centuries after Edward Jenner demonstrated the potential of a vaccine. It took much more than advances in medical knowledge to eradicate smallpox. It took social architecture—the design of a complex, global human system. Nearly a quarter million people coordinated their efforts, from researchers and politicians in big cities to health care workers and volunteers in remote villages.

And it took one man's belief in what could be.

Today, we take this and other equally amazing accomplishments for granted, as we hurry to the next contest.

IDEAS
LEAD THE WAY

The philosopher Arthur Schopenhauer observed that every new idea passes through three stages. "First, it is ridiculed. Second, it is violently opposed. Third, it is accepted as being self-evident."

Take another example: women's right to vote. In the United States, it has taken less than 100 years to cycle through the three stages. The suffragists of the early 20th century were accused of mental imbalance, even insanity. Today, it seems absurd that women were ever barred from the ballot box, and the weight of public opinion worldwide favors universal suffrage.

New possibilities have developed from this shift in thinking. Women are increasingly represented among the ranks of elected leaders. And at this writing, women leaders and grassroots women's groups stand poised to shift Africa's fate from victim to victor.

It's ideas such as universal voting rights—and intentional acts to bring them to fruition—that have led the way in our civilization. It may seem that the march of history has been a succession of solving problems and overcoming obstacles. It's easy to subscribe to the notion that impersonal forces and trends govern the course of human events, and we are helplessly propelled into a future not of our making.

Is there another way to see it?

Could it be that bringing new realities to life is a creative act, an act of imagination? Could it be an act of volition, rather than simple necessity?

When Rosa Parks refused to move to the back of the bus, was it because she needed a seat? "People always say that I didn't give up my seat because I was tired," she said. "But that isn't true. I was not tired physically, or no more tired than I usually was at the end of a working day. No, the only tired I was, was tired of giving in."

Parks had been a civil rights activist for more than a decade before that historic day. When she kept her seat on the bus, she acted with will and intention to create a new future. She was part of a far-flung network of people who had joined together to bring new meaning to the ideals of justice and freedom, to redefine what was possible for American society, to attempt the impossible.

There was nothing modest about their undertaking. "I have a dream," Martin Luther King, Jr. proclaimed from the steps of the Lincoln Memorial. In that same speech, he invoked "the fierce urgency of now" and decried "the tranquilizing drug of gradualism." Only from such a bold stance could he have uttered the words that echoed around the world and still ring in our hearts.

When we live into such a new way of being, our idea of what is possible is forever altered. As Oliver Wendell Holmes put it, "One's mind, once stretched by a new idea, never regains its original dimensions."

And a society, once reimagined, grows toward that ideal, as a plant stretches upward toward the sun.

THREE

WHERE DOES OUR DESTINY COME FROM?

JUST *TALK?*
THAT'S ENOUGH?

So how does it happen, this opening of new doors, this continual redefinition of what we believe the world can be?

It takes place in conversations. "Just talk" has always been the path to reinvent the world.

"Back in college, I'd go to a women's consciousness-raising group every week at the YWCA across the street from the university," Pam told me as we were working on this book. "It didn't seem like much—a dozen women sitting in a circle, talking. But it changed my world."

"We talked about jobs and sex and politics, about history and housework and love," she continued. "We told each other stories about our own lives and the truths we found in our most personal experiences. We dissected language and questioned society's rules. We talked about the books we were reading—*The Second Sex; The Feminine Mystique; Our Bodies, Our Selves.*"

They also relived the stories of other women, Pam told me. The heroic women of the past, like those who had won the right to vote a mere half-century earlier, at the same time Margaret Sanger was championing reproductive freedom.

"Most of all," she said, "I learned for the first time that I wasn't alone. I found myself united with strong women, past and present, who shared my desire to be free individuals. In their company, I learned who I could be and what I could stand for."

"There was no going back."

All across the United States, and beyond, countless women held similar conversations, and sparked a revolution. By "just talking," they created new agreements about social norms. They changed forever what it means to be a woman and what it means to be a man; indeed, what it means to be human. What seemed to be private, personal interactions permanently changed the way we see each other.

Those changes have become so interwoven in our culture that it's now difficult to fully grasp their significance. Let me touch on just one aspect that stands out for me right now. My mother died when I was 8 years old. I learned much later that my father cried himself to sleep every night after her death. But at the time, he never let me know that, never spoke to me of the depth of his grief. The minister who told me of my mother's death assured me, as my father sat by, "Son, it's OK to cry." Instead, I followed my father's stoic example.

Today, it's hard for me to imagine that was once the way men were expected to be. When I watch an emotional movie with my son, he'll often sneak a glance at me, knowing there's a good chance he'll get to see me teary.

In the space of just one generation, the genius has been let out of the bottle, and our world has been transformed.

CAN ONE DINNER CONVERSATION CHANGE THE WORLD?

Peter Robinson tells a surprising story of his days as a presidential speechwriter.

Robinson visited Berlin in May 1987 to gather material for a speech Ronald Reagan would give a few weeks later. He recalls being briefed by an American diplomat. "Don't mention the Wall," he was told, "it will upset people. And besides, people here have gotten used to it."

At dinner with a dozen Berliners, Robinson related what he had been told. "Is it true?" he asked. "Have you gotten used to the wall?" Robinson writes of the conversation that ensued:

> The Elzes and their guests glanced at each other uneasily. I assumed I'd proved to be just the sort of brash, tactless American the diplomat was afraid the president might send. Then one of the men raised his arm and pointed. "My sister lives 20 miles in that direction," he said. "I haven't seen her in more than two decades. Do you think I can get used to that?"
>
> Another man spoke. Each morning, he explained, on his way to work he walked past the same guard tower. Each morning the same soldier gazed down at him through binoculars. "That soldier and I speak the same language. We share the same history. But one of us is a zookeeper and the other is an animal, and I am never certain which is which."

Our hostess broke in. A gracious woman, she had grown angry. Her face was red. She made a fist with one hand, then pounded it into the palm of the other. "If this man Gorbachev is serious with his talk of *glasnost* and *perestroika*," she said, "he can prove it. He can get rid of this wall."

Those Berliners saw a reality far different from that visible to the American diplomats stationed in the same city.

When Robinson returned to Washington, he made Frau Elz's comment the central passage of the speech. The State Department, the National Security Council, the Secretary of State, and many others in the administration tried to squelch it, calling the demand to tear down the wall provocative and naïve.

Reagan was adamant: It was the right thing to say. He had listened to the actual experiences and desires of Berliners—rather than to the professional's calls to be "realistic." And he divined an underground stream that was soon to rush to the surface. Soon after, he stood in front of the Berlin wall and delivered a challenge. "Mr. Gorbachev, tear down this wall!"

Two and half years later, the border between East and West Berlin was opened, the Wall demolished. Today, only paving stones and small sections of wall mark where it once stood.

Countless conversations and actions contributed to that momentous event, and many accounts could be told of those days.

Still, I am struck by how a single dinner conversation — and the willingness to listen to it—may have shaped our sense of what was possible and influenced the course of history.

WORDS
CREATE WORLDS

How does talk play such a central role in creating the future?

The answer is at once simple and profound: It's by talking together that we agree on what is real and what is good, what we want and what can stir our minds and excite our hearts.

In our conversations—and especially in the stories we tell about what has been and what is—we create what we desire and what we believe the future can be. We draw from more than face-to-face conversations and we are fed by the dynamic interplay among all the ways we tell stories and create social agreements: sending an e-mail to a friend, watching a television show, reading a book.

This phenomenon has been called the *social construction of reality*. In essence, we construct our current sense of the way things are, the way things can be, and even the way things *ought* to be. In the process, we create frameworks that allow us to see some things and not others. Much of what we can see depends upon our context: the time and the place where we live.

This idea is in contrast to the popular notion that *individual* idiosyncrasies of personality or perception are the only reason people see things differently.

Here's an example: I can almost always find value in situations that others consider dismal. Many people would chalk that up to my "positive" personality, an inherent tendency to see the world through "rose-colored glasses." And maybe there is something in my nature that leans me in this direction, although I can also skillfully identify, and gripe about, things I wish were different.

There's more going on here than positive thinking, happy-faced living, or some individual's peculiarity: I've spent years *learning* to construct the world this way. I've had practice in countless conversations with colleagues, teachers, clients, therapists, friends. I've learned from books, articles, workshops, lectures. From relationships with people who share a set of beliefs about what's important and what's desirable. And even from relationships with people who hold views that anger me.

Along the way, certain aspects of myself have been brought forward, and others have been left in the background. My more critical self is still in the wings, waiting for his cue. But the constructs I've developed (I hope I've *chosen* to develop most of them) have allowed other parts of me to take center stage.

In similar ways, each of us learns how to make sense of the world and of ourselves. We use our mental models to actively reach out and *construct* the world, rather than just passively perceive what's "out there." For most of us, most of the time, this process of making meaning happens beyond our conscious awareness.

Rarely do we examine the frameworks and mental models we have created, our habitual patterns of thought and speech.

Even more rarely do we see that we have a choice in the matter.

Understanding this dynamic opens up significant new potential for social change. It's a liberating prospect: We have many more choices available to us than we usually believe. We can choose, consciously and intentionally, to change our social agreements by changing our conversations, the language we use, the stories we tell. We can open up new possibilities for society.

Popular thought is that we get results through "less talk, more action!" But that's a sure way to perpetuate the status quo, or at best to get incremental improvements. Talk is essential if we are to create fresh ideas and new expectations, and foster the creativity and social innovation that will spark the futures we want. A new maxim is in order: "More talk, bolder action!"

As we're beginning to see, it makes a big difference what the talk is about.

THE UNSTOPPABLE POWER
OF EXPECTATIONS

Our images and expectations about the future may well be the most fateful social agreement we create through our dialogue.

My friend Dr. Charles Elliott, when he was dean of Trinity Hall at Cambridge University, was reviewing an application for admission one afternoon. Although he'd left his glasses at home that day, it looked like those who had interviewed the applicant and perused her records had signed off on admitting her. "If she was good enough for them," he thought, "she's good enough for me." And he signed to admit her.

"Four years later," Charles told one of our workshops at the college, "I heard a knock at my door. A young lady had climbed the narrow two flights of stairs to my office to thank me. She said, 'Dean Elliott, when no one else would believe in me, you believed in me. With grades like mine, I didn't belong at Cambridge, but I figured that if you believed in me, I could do the work. Thanks to you, I will be graduated *summa cum laude* later today.'"

This story always reminds me of the people who have believed in me over the years. I have a hunch everyone has those memories. Perhaps there's been a time when someone saw something in you that you didn't see in yourself. They saw a seed, a potential, and it made a lasting difference in your life. As well, the roles have been reversed when you believed in someone and it made a difference for them (even though you may have never known the influence you had).

These personal experiences bring alive what social scientists have found through decades of research: that the expectations we hold—our images of others—have a profound effect.

In one classic design, researchers told teachers that certain students had unusually high potential for success in school. The children were in fact selected at random, rather than for any innate abilities. Several months later, the chosen few were surpassing their classmates due to the kind of attention, subtle as it may have been, that they had received as a result of their teacher's expectations. The students' self-images had been altered and they had responded with increased effort and focus. Believing themselves to have more talent, they performed better than they would have otherwise.

This well-documented phenomenon has been called the "Pygmalion effect," a reference to George Bernard Shaw's play of the same name (which later became the musical "My Fair Lady"). In the play, Eliza Dolittle, a Cockney flower girl who has been transformed into a duchess, gives us a more colorful explanation.

> You see, really and truly, apart from the things anyone can pick up (the dressing and the proper way of speaking and so on), the difference between a lady and a flower girl is not how she behaves but how she's treated. I shall always be a flower girl to Professor Higgins, because he always treats me as a flower girl, and always will, but I know I can be a lady to you because you always treat me as a lady, and always will.

Whether we prefer to take our cues from personal experience, experimental evidence, or literature, it is apparent that the images we hold of other people have effects that are both genuine and significant.

If our beliefs about people can be that powerful, the implications are intriguing, to say the least. It's an energizing conclusion: Little about human development or behavior is predetermined or unchangeable. Just as the future is open to our influence, so are societies, organizations, and individuals.

"But Jim, 'images' are no more than foggy self-delusions," a friend once said to me. "These studies just show it's hard for people to be objective about reality and take action based on facts."

Is my friend right? Would we be better off if we were more clear-eyed about "the truth" and more "objective" about ourselves and others?

Hardly.

I see in all of this not a human defect, but an extraordinary human gift: The ability to create a picture of a distant reality and to bring that expectation into the present moment, as if it already exists. Doing so in a conscious, intentional manner—based on choosing to see the best— is an act of leadership, a creative act that supports our highest aspirations for ourselves and society.

This is the approach of the artist, and of Churchill.

EVERYDAY TALK
IS FATEFUL

Expectations and pictures of the future are just as fateful for any human system, whether an individual, organization, community, or even a whole culture.

In his sweeping study of Western civilization, the Dutch sociologist and business leader Frederick Polak argues that the image we hold of the future is the single most important factor in understanding the evolution of society.

"The rise and fall of images of the future precedes or accompanies the rise and fall of cultures," Polak writes. "As long as a society's image is positive and flourishing, the flower of culture is in full bloom. Once the image begins to decay and lose its vitality, however, the culture does not long survive."

In a similar vein, the ancient wisdom of the Old Testament holds that "Where there is no vision, the people perish."

Anthropologists have found this to be literally true. Certain societies have actually given up and allowed themselves to die when their images of the future have become too bleak. The depopulation of Melanesia early in the nineteenth century, as well as the loss of interest by the Marquesan Islanders in having children, are two examples. "In the second case it appears that the islanders simply gave up when, in the face of inroads from white traders and missionaries, everything that gave them hope and a sense of value was eroded," writes cultural anthropologist Ernest Becker.

Today's popular wisdom is that "vision" is contained in some official statement created and handed down by a designated leader, or by a small leadership group. We look to top elected leaders for a nation's vision. We demand that the CEO deliver vision to an organization.

Leaders certainly can influence the image of the future held by the people they lead, as Churchill did in 1940. But the guiding image I'm talking about here is much more than the proclamations of a single leader, however powerful or charismatic. It's the picture of tomorrow that is shaped in everyday conversations and relationships among the people in the system. Our belief about what is possible develops around the water cooler, rather than solely in the board room. It's created in the dialogue that constantly runs through the circle of people who will bring the vision to life.

The *quality* of this dialogue, these everyday conversations, is crucial to the future. Those seemingly insignificant exchanges add up. They determine whether our collective guiding image is vibrant and alive, or tired and listless.

We've arrived at a conclusion that may seem surprising: the words we speak each day, often without thought, can be of historic import. "Just talking" in an intentional and thoughtful way, fully aware of the power of our words, may be the most revolutionary activity we can pursue.

FOUR

THE COURAGE TO CHOOSE OUR STORIES

WINGS
OF HOPE

Gene Sparling tells of the rediscovery of the ivory-billed woodpecker, long thought to have been lost forever.

An amateur naturalist, Sparling had paddled his kayak into Arkansas' Bayou DeView, hoping to see 1,000-year-old trees. "It was a magical place," he recently told a packed auditorium. "Deep and magical, with trees that were very old. I put my paddle down across my lap and leaned back to enjoy the moment, feeling lucky and grateful. And I made a mental note that I wanted to remember that feeling and hold onto it."

"Right at that moment, a very large woodpecker flew toward me," Sparling continued. "It pulled up when it saw me, giving me a glimpse of white-edged wings."

The ivory-billed woodpecker flashed through his mind, but he dismissed the thought as absurd. Everyone knew they'd been extinct since 1944, his whole life, so he couldn't have seen one. But this woodpecker was really big, and its wings had white edges, so it had to be an ivory-billed.

"Around and around, the same thoughts ran," he said, "wearing a groove in my brain."

When he returned from the trip, he posted a report on his canoe club's Web site. He wasn't going to do anything more with the sighting, but a woman who read about it urged him on, telling him he had a duty to report what he had seen.

A 14-month search for the bird ensued. Members of the search team obtained some barely recognizable video, flashes of wide, white-edged wings amid the trees.

Those brief glimpses caught people's imaginations and sparked ambitious plans to protect and restore the vast expanse of forested swamps that the ivory-billed woodpecker once called home.

"I learned two great lessons from this experience," he continued. "I learned to believe that the most wonderful things can happen in this world. And I learned that ordinary people can have an extraordinary impact, beyond our wildest dreams."

As Sparling concluded his tale, the excited crowd leaped up to give him an enthusiastic standing ovation.

THE SEDUCTIVE
LAW OF GRAVITY

There was one more speaker on the program after Gene Sparling: a trustee from one of the event's sponsors.

"She had a different story to tell: that we need hopeful tales like Gene's so we can get through all the tragedies that life brings us," says a colleague who was there. "And then she detailed a long list of such troubles. My mind filled with painful images. I felt sick to my stomach."

"People clapped at the end," my colleague continues, "but from what I could see, the energy of the standing ovation was gone. It sure was for me."

It's natural, and can be useful, to interpret a euphoric experience by putting it into the context of everyday life, as this speaker did. But so often we treat the high point as if it were the exception. We see our highs as fleeting moments, not to be trusted.

We let gravity pull us down from the mountaintop to the apparent safety of base camp.

IS CYNICISM
JUST A STORY WE TELL?

Gene Sparling says that he almost let the amazing gift of the ivory-billed woodpecker slip away because he "was too skeptical and cynical and afraid of being called a fool. I thought it was up to someone else to save the bird, that I wasn't worthy of the task."

Many of us share that skeptical and cynical outlook. In the course of just a few decades, it has become the dominant mindset. For many people, withdrawal from public life has followed.

The bitter divisiveness of American politics is just one example of this pervasive cultural phenomenon.

After all, it's easy to look at the past several decades and extract a dismal tale of official wrongdoing. The Kennedy assassination and the conspiracy theories that surrounded it. The excesses of the FBI under Hoover. Official lies told to justify the Vietnam War. Watergate and the first U.S. president to resign.

We tell and retell accounts of these events, and many since, with an intense focus on just one story line: powerful people have repeatedly violated the public trust. It's only natural that our sense of betrayal would grow and extend to other leaders and institutions, including those in the social sector.

Cynicism is an understandable response to that reality. Indeed, in such a context the cynic's expression of a truth can even seem like a breath of fresh air.

There's something else at work here. I'd also suggest that cynicism is a cover for people whose idealism has been buried under disappointment and frustration. When we feel our high hopes for society have been dashed, it may be healthy self-protection to tone down our dreams, to become reserved and skeptical.

But the cost is great when mistrust becomes the prevailing way of life, when society as a whole experiences a generalized loss of belief in people and in institutions of all kinds. It's one thing to hold a healthy skepticism and to question authority. It's quite another to allow cynicism to become so dominant a way of meeting the world that it limits what we believe is possible for humanity.

This kind of atmosphere puts a damper on creativity, imagination, and achievement. Little breathing room is left for passions, hopes, and dreams, which get picked apart, dismissed, even ridiculed. Yet, as we've seen, those very ingredients are the foundation of a vibrant civilization.

Different stories can be told if we turn our attention to what the past tells us about what we're made of, who we are as a people. We may be surprised to find that the very events often cited as evidence of social decline can instead be seen as our proudest moments, recounted as times when our democratic institutions prevailed, a free press exposed official lies, and ordinary people's voices were heard.

What options would open to us if we chose to tell those stories? How might that choice sustain the vitality of public life?

As I've said before, we could spend a lot of time exploring which accounts of our past are most "true" or "real." I have a different question in mind: Of all the stories we could choose to relate, which are most useful in creating the world we want?

SEARCHING FOR
A SIGN OF LIFE

A chapter of a large international organization had just laid off staff due to a looming budget deficit—the first layoffs in its history. You can imagine the talk in the halls about how dire the situation was, how tenuous the future looked.

At the same time, a small team was preparing for a staff retreat that would kick off a strategic planning process. One member of the team argued, with considerable passion, that time must be allowed for people to vent and grieve, out of respect to the staff's feelings in this difficult time.

That's the conventional wisdom: We must "meet people where they are" and give them a chance to say what's on their minds. It seems the honest thing to do. Only when all of the difficulties have been confronted and handled can we start looking toward the future.

Makes all the sense in the world, but I feel weary just writing that, much less going through it. What we have here is the metaphor of organization as machine: All we have to do is fix what's broken and everything will run perfectly, or at least well enough to chug along.

What if we approached our personal health that way, finding every possible fault with our bodies, focusing on fixing all the defects before we let ourselves start to do the health-promoting things that will make the biggest difference in our lives? We'd be so preoccupied with our hangnails that we'd never get around to riding a bike, meditating, or eating well. We might even worry ourselves to death.

What's more, we just assume that being authentic and honest requires sharing every thought that crosses our minds, including angry ones. Instead, research shows that such venting only escalates feelings of anger and often does little to move people forward.

What happens when we set aside the standard practices that require us to identify and fix problems as the first order of business? What if we ask people to talk about their best moments and highest aspirations, rather than their grievances, even when they are in situations that appear to be difficult? What if we treated the organization as a living system and searched for what gives it life?

The retreat was designed from that unusual stance. The facilitator opened the session by asking staff to tell stories of recent successes, those projects and accomplishments that they felt represented their best achievements.

The planning team had expected only a handful of people would speak. To everyone's surprise, dozens of people stood to talk about their high points. Several eager hands were still in the air as the facilitator reluctantly moved to the next part of the agenda.

Susan, a much-admired staff member, had arrived at the retreat in a skeptical frame of mind. As the meeting came to a close the following afternoon, she quietly remarked to the people at her table, "Now I *know* we can do the impossible."

Perhaps the retreat would have worked better for some if time had been provided to air complaints. I expect there were some who felt the "real issues" had been swept under the rug. But they were few in number, even fewer than the retreat's planners had imagined. And perhaps even they began to experience a different reality as they heard their colleagues' stories.

The way I see it, the meeting was designed to show respect for people like Susan, those who have in them the kind of energy that moves a group forward (perhaps just waiting to be released). What would have been gained by subjecting her, and the many like her, to an airing of grievances? What would have been gained by sweeping under the rug their accomplishments, their pride in their work, their hopes and dreams?

A group always has a finite amount of time to do its work. So it's crucial to ask: what will move us forward both quickly and effectively? Do we spend time dissecting and attempting to solve all the problems we can find, or do we move directly to a higher level?

YOU STILL THINK YOU MUST ADDRESS A PROBLEM HEAD-ON?

Rosemary Cairns shares an instructive tale from one of her experiences working all over the world: a meeting in the remote city of Yellowknife, in Canada's Northwest Territories. Like many such meetings convened by the government, it was a mix of aboriginal and non-aboriginal people.

"I noticed how many of the aboriginal people weren't speaking," Rosemary says. "There seemed to be a certain tone to the comments of many of the non-aboriginal people (although they probably wouldn't have noticed it). It had to do with that sort of *realistic* approach—let's look at how things really are, which in so many aboriginal communities seems to be a catalogue of non-achievement, a wasting of resources, and an unspoken agreement that it will take a long time before things change."

"In my earlier years, I would have probably said that out loud and alienated three-quarters of the room," she continues. "But one of the great things about aging is that—like aboriginal elders—I've taken to telling stories instead."

Feeling quite nervous, she says, Rosemary told the group a story of what had happened in Old Crow, a re-

mote aboriginal community in the neighboring northern Yukon territory, during World War II. The people
of Old Crow had heard on the radio about the children
who were orphaned as a result of the bombing of London.
They placed a high value on children and family, so they
wanted to make a difference. Despite their remoteness
and comparative poverty, the few hundred people living
in Old Crow collected about 700 dollars, a very large sum
for them. They sent the money to the British High Commissioner in Ottawa, who sent it on to London.

The commissioner actually came to visit Old Crow to
thank them for this contribution. They passed the hat and
raised another 70 or 80 dollars.

"There was dead silence after I had finished telling this
story, a story that I believed described the kind of people who were in the room with me," Rosemary says. "I
wondered whether I'd made a mistake and thought that I
must have sounded naive."

But in telling the story, Rosemary had challenged the
unspoken assumptions underlying the conversations in
the meeting. The story she had chosen contained irrefut-
able proof of the capabilities of native communities. That
provided a new ground, a new social agreement about
who could speak and what they could talk about. And
soon a young aboriginal man raised his hand and began
to tell of his work in a small community on the other side
of the lake.

"He spoke from his heart," says Rosemary, "from his
authentic experience." That he spoke and how he spoke
was even more important than what he said. He opened
up the meeting to participation by many of the aboriginal

people who had been silent up until then, and to a different level of discussion about development.

One person's carefully chosen story can interrupt the
status quo and create new options for a group.

THE COURAGE TO START
A NEW CONVERSATION

Imagine yourself in a village in Nepal, the second poorest
country in the world, where most years even the farmers
go hungry for a few months.

That's where Tricia Lustig, a British consultant, found
herself several years ago. She'd been invited there by the
village headman to work with the villagers, and began her
work by asking them if they wanted to tell stories of times
they had achieved something together in the village.

"The villagers did not understand what we'd accomplish by talking about what had gone well (instead of
things that were wrong)," says Tricia. But then she asked
them to dream: What kind of a village do you want for
your children and grandchildren?

"That began to get great excitement going," Tricia says.
"As soon as we started to talk about how we might *do*
this ourselves, the energy started to dissipate. There was
some reluctance to commit to doing things themselves —
to move from being victims to being leaders."

Then Pasang Lama, a subsistence farmer with but a few
acres — a man who could neither read nor write — stood
up to address the villagers.

"We've been bloody lazy," he proclaimed. "For the past 40 years we have been holding our hands out for aid, and what do we get? I'll tell you what we get: We get fights. We can't agree on anything, and we don't feel good about our village or ourselves.

"Forty years ago we did a lot together because there was no one else to help us, and you know what? We were proud of what we did! We were proud of our village!"

Silence.

"Are any of you proud now?" he concluded. "No? Well, let's work together and be proud again!"

"After Pasang spoke, it became amazing," Tricia says. "People stood up and offered the most impossible things. One man, Mr. Bal, was blind and could not provide for his family himself. But his wife ran a teashop. He said she made 600 rupees a month and he would pledge a whole month of her wages to building the new school. She was there too, nodding enthusiastically. He cried as he said, 'our future is our children.'"

Three years later, Tricia returned to the village and saw that the school they had reckoned would take five years to build was already finished and in use. Today there are eight teachers, two paid for by the villagers themselves. There's even a village bank.

All from a shift in the dialogue.

When I bring up these kinds of ideas with folks, they often nod in agreement, and then sometimes gently tell me that *their* situation is so bad that it has to be an exception. "Jim, this all sounds good," one person said. "But you've got to understand that the problems in *my* community truly are terrible and just have to be confronted head-on."

I've heard much the same from others about their organization, cause, or even the world.

And yet, my experience has been that even in systems that seem "dysfunctional," the patient is still alive. In *every* situation, we have the opportunity to wonder: What animates this place, these people? What sustains their life, perhaps in what seems like a small way? ("To see things in the seed, that is genius," wrote the Chinese philosopher Lao Tzu, founder of Taoism.) If people rigorously and systematically focus on their health and vitality, what path might they find to enliven themselves even more?

The choice to take this stance is always available to us. But more often, we feel pressed for immediate action and quick results, so we fall back on our habitual patterns. We rush to get to the problem and pass by opportunities to foster the greater awareness that inspires greater action.

What happens if we slow down (just a little)? What if, as we prepare for our many meetings, we made an inspiring dialogue part of the agenda? Might we start to legitimize conversations that are positive, personal, reflective, and genuine—the kind of discourse that energizes people, connects them with others, and nurtures the seeds of human potential?

That sounds attractive, at least to me. And yet, having said all of this, I've found that people often shrink from applying these ideas.

It takes courage to break from our routines and bring our ideals, hopes, and dreams out into the open; to make them legitimate topics of conversation; to shift our sense of what is and what is possible by changing the way we talk about it.

It takes courage to reclaim our power to change the world.

FIVE

WHAT QUESTIONS
DARE WE ASK?

THE POWER OF
THE QUESTION

On a family vacation in the early 1940s, Dad's busy snapping photos for the family album. "Why can't I see the picture now?" his three-year–old daughter asks, and an industry is born.

The dad was Edwin Land, founder of Polaroid. His daughter's innocent question inspired the invention of instant photography, a cultural phenomenon for half a century.

A child's natural curiosity and freedom from preconceived ideas let her look beyond the obvious and come up with such a "silly" question, the kind of question that just might open new doors.

Some of us manage to carry that openness into adulthood. (Francis Crick and James Watson, who discovered the structure of DNA, would often sit over beers, entertaining Crick's intentionally naive questions. They found in that exercise important clues to their discovery.)

More often, we learn to discount such curiosity. We learn the value of appearing to be authoritative, decisive, knowledgeable—especially if we're in leadership positions.

And when we do ask questions, many of us change the kinds of questions we ask. In board rooms and management meetings, we're taken more seriously if we ask critical questions that send an unspoken message: I know what I'm doing.

Less often do we ask unusual questions that go beyond the status quo. But those are the very questions that will move us forward.

"My greatest strength as a consultant," said Peter Drucker, the father of modern management, "is to be ignorant and ask a few questions."

Or as Egyptian novelist Naguib Mahfouz put it, "You can tell whether a man is clever by his answers. You can tell whether a man is wise by his questions."

WHICH QUESTIONS ARE BETTER?

The first question we ask plants the seeds of the future.

"What's your heartburn issue in this community—the one thing that could keep you awake at night?" a Jacksonville, Florida, consultant asked community leaders during interviews for a social services agency.

At the same time, her colleague, Kathy Wells, was conducting similar interviews for an organization devoted to elders. Kathy chose a different question: "What has been a high point for you in the life of this community—a time when joining with others on behalf of the greater good had been especially satisfying?"

Both projects were successful. The initiative Kathy designed was extraordinarily successful. It laid the groundwork for an inquiry designed to change forever what it means to grow older in society, to which we'll return in the next chapter.

For now, I'd like to underscore the vital difference between the questions asked by these two consultants.

As we've seen, in every human system, there is a tacit social agreement about what makes people tick, what's important, and how the world works. Naturally, those understandings shape the questions that are asked.

Kathy's question about a high point assumed that people would have uplifting memories of working with others in the community. It also assumed that something useful could be learned by studying the best of those experiences.

Her colleague stood in a very different place. She chose a question that assumed people had big problems on their minds and that it would be important to focus attention on those.

"I thought hard about what I was going to ask, because I knew the question would set the stage," Kathy told me. "I really wanted my question to enliven people, to locate and develop their energy."

(Someone once asked me, "Jim, you travel so much; how is it that you have so much energy?" The question reinforced the kind of energy she was talking about. I would have felt less of that energy had she asked, "Doesn't so much travel tire you?")

Kathy worked from the insight that all questions are filled with unspoken assumptions. They're "loaded." More than that: The questions we choose to ask largely determine the kinds of stories people will tell in response. As we've already seen, the very act of telling those stories will shape their (and our) realities.

This has been named the simultaneity principle. And it's a far cry from the way most consultants study and work with human systems. More often, questions are thought of as neutral tools for fact-finding. Researchers strive to ask unbiased questions that they believe will give them an objective picture of what's going on. When they're done with this detached analysis, they proceed to create plans for action or change, blissfully unaware that their very questions have already affected the way people see things, including the energy they have for whatever plan might ensue.

When we understand the simultaneity principle, we can intentionally ask questions that create more of what we want. We can build in a bias for action, right from the start.

We can ask questions that carry assumptions of competence and capability, and the seeds of confidence and courage.

A CONTRARIAN DISCOVERY
UNCOVERS HIDDEN POWER

In 1980, a young graduate student at Case Western Reserve University's management school was hard at work on his dissertation. He had selected the Cleveland Clinic, one of the world's largest and most respected medical centers, as a place to study the questions on his mind.

As a graduate student, he became thoroughly familiar with the best thinking then current in his field. Under the spell of the late 20th-century critical mindset, the academic study of organizations (as well as popular notions about management) was entirely focused on problems and deficits, pathology and dysfunction.

So the student set out to discover (more accurately, to diagnose) what might be ailing the Cleveland Clinic. He found something entirely different. And what he discovered has shaken many long-entrenched beliefs about organizations, and even about people.

Instead of finding a sick organization at the Cleveland Clinic, his questions led him to sources of life and energy: cooperation, innovation, egalitarian governance. That didn't fit into the deficit models he'd learned in graduate school. So he proposed an entirely different study: an investigation into the factors that contributed to the clinic functioning at its best, the forces that gave it life. It was the first large-scale inquiry based on such a model.

The student was David Cooperrider, who we'll meet again in a few pages. His experience at the Cleveland Clinic was the first step in developing a promising new way of advancing people and organizations: appreciative inquiry.

The term may well be new to you. And if you're at all like me, you may be cringing at the thought of yet one more management buzzword. It's a good bit more than that. I've become convinced that appreciative inquiry offers tremendous potential to promote the growth and vitality of human systems, especially those devoted to the common good.

We've already seen the value of *inquiry,* asking questions because we want to learn something new. This kind of inquiry revives the sense of wonder that opens up new options. Thanks to David, I have come to value my presence as an everlasting beginner far more highly than any expertise I might offer. As the Zen master Shunryo Suzuki-Roshi put it, "In the beginner's mind there are many possibilities, but in the expert's there are few."

What about *appreciation?* In an age of criticism and even cynicism, that may sound a bit "soft." But in fact appreciation is an unexpectedly powerful act.

When we appreciate something or someone, we often mean we're grateful. That's fine, as a start. We can also mean we're recognizing and liking the qualities of something, treasuring it, valuing it, seeking to understand it fully, as when we appreciate art.

It gets better. When we pause to appreciate something (or someone), the object of our regard can actually *increase in value,* as a house or business might appreciate. Recall how our belief in an individual exerts an influence vastly greater than we usually recognize. We saw this in the Pygmalion effect—the higher achievement that often follows from being held in high regard—and in what happened for the student at Cambridge when she felt someone had believed in her.

On a much larger scale, remember Frederick Polak's conclusion that a bright image of the future is vital to the destiny of a civilization. As we'll soon see, appreciation is the most effective way to generate such images, and the confidence to bring them to fruition.

SIX

MIGHT WE EVEN REFRAME THE HUMAN CONDITION?

WHAT ABOUT
MEETING NEEDS?

More than 25 years ago, in a book written for civic leaders, I boldly proclaimed that "organizations have no needs."

"*People* have needs, *communities* have needs," I wrote, "but organizations have no needs. Organizations have *solutions.*" As you may guess, I've since come to see that people and communities are also laden with resources, and to question the entire notion of "needs."

This is an unusual stance among people who work with social sector organizations and social causes. The norm is to be acutely aware of the needs of our communities and the world—needs that often seem endless and overwhelming. It's far more difficult for us to see that the capabilities of the world are also without limit.

Indeed, many people talk as if needs are the only reason to act, whether at the personal or global level. Just as we're drawn to what's wrong and what's missing, we tend to identify needs in people and situations, and then allow our sense of necessity to determine (and limit) what we can do.

Here's an everyday example: I find myself saying "I need to go to the drugstore" or "I need to get this worked out," even though I know these are wants or desires, rather than "needs." It's as if necessity must be proven in order to justify acting on what I want.

The same habitual pattern permeates most thinking about the advancement of society.

I feel sad as I write this, for a focus on needs as the place to start usually gives us a diminished view of life:

just enough to get by, rather than the world we most de-sire. It's based on a sense of deficit and scarcity, rather than aspiration. Although addressing needs is a worthy and honorable task, that stance may in fact prevent us from seeing much greater possibilities for the human con-dition.

Even more, it's a small step from identifying needs to defining certain individuals and certain peoples as "needy" (and thus deficient). For what we call a need is nothing more than a set of assumptions about what is missing *and* about who has the power and resources to do something about it.

That lesson was brought home to me when I went to Nairobi to work with trustees and staff from relief and development organizations in Uganda, Ethiopia, Tan-zania, and Kenya. Toward the end of our time together, folks separated into groups by country and planned what they would do when they returned home. Three of the four groups decided (unknown to one another) to work on "the problem of street children."

Who could deny the neediness of children who had no homes, no families?

Well, that had me scratching my head for a while. I hadn't prepared myself for how my "appreciative" work could apply to this situation that weighed so heavily on their hearts. Besides, what did I know about street chil-dren?

Then it came to me. What if *I* were a child of the streets? What would that be like? What kind of person might I be?

That shift in perspective allowed me to ask the group: "What are street children like as individuals? What do they have going for them? What capabilities and assets do they have?"

Beginning with such questions, we were able to see a resourceful group of young people who live by their wits, creativity, and tenacity. We saw that, no matter how daunting the circumstances and how little the hope, street children somehow continue to have a will to live. Learning about the vitality of these courageous children, and where that vitality comes from, would be a worthy pursuit.

So the pathway was obvious: an inquiry into what the street children had to teach the well-meaning adults about hope and promise. As a group, I think we did rather well in shifting our "deficit eyes" toward strength and possibility.

One of the country teams chose a different inquiry. The group from Tanzania decided to inquire into what stimulates the philanthropic impulse. They went on to raise U.S. $1.5 million during their annual campaign—*within* the country, an astounding accomplishment. What they learned about themselves, their resourcefulness and power, may have been even more important than the money they raised. (Imagine how different the outcome might have been had they started with a traditional "needs assessment.")

What happens when we question the entire framework of needs and needy people, and instead turn our attention to the capabilities inherent in people?

TRUSTING
EACH OTHER

On an ordinary Tuesday morning in 1998, in the small town of Jonesboro, Arkansas, two boys came to school armed with high-powered rifles. Just 11 and 13 years old, they opened fire on their classmates, left four children dead and 10 wounded, and killed an English teacher who had tried to shield a student.

As the heartbreaking news spread, everyone in the community—indeed, in the world—struggled to make sense of such a bizarre and frightening act. "Babies killing babies," as one mother put it.

The unimaginable happened again a year later at Columbine High School in Colorado. Two teenage boys smuggled in backpacks and duffle bags crammed with sawed-off shotguns, semi-automatic weapons, and nearly a hundred bombs. In less than an hour, they shot dead 12 students and a teacher, and left 24 wounded. If two of their bombs had gone off as planned, the devastation could have killed all 2,000-plus students. The boys ended the massacre by committing suicide.

The corridors at Columbine High soon filled with boxes of teddy bears, letters and cards, and other expressions of sympathy.

"It felt good, but we never really went through them," recalled Matt, who was a senior at Columbine when I met him two years later. "What we paid attention to was one item. And that's still on the wall in the school: a poster created by the kids at Jonesboro and signed by all of them."

Matt was with a group of high school students from Columbine, Jonesboro, and Paducah (the site of an earlier school shooting) who had gathered at Ferncliff, a Presbyterian camp in Little Rock, Arkansas.

Five of the students met to articulate what they had learned from their experiences. Some had been injured in the gunfire, some had lost friends, all had been affected emotionally. They wanted to figure out how to guide themselves and others in dealing with future tragedies. Using the approach we've been talking about, they were asked to tell stories of when they had been at their *best* in the dark days of the shootings.

It may seem odd, or even unfeeling, to ask people to talk about their best moments—their high points—when they have suffered through such horror. Yet there were more such moments than even I could have imagined.

These young people shared and relived astonishing stories of compassion, of heroism, of strength. They came to understand the conditions that had supported their strengths. That knowledge, carefully harvested from the truths of their own experiences, led them to develop two key principles to guide them in the future.

> *The Jonesboro poster principle.* Just "being there" with us is as important as words—maybe more important.

"We call it 'accompaniment,'" David Gill, the camp's director, told me. "I can't make everything better, but I can accompany you on your journey. People in the early stages of trauma do not need to hear 'It will be okay.' The mere presence of youth who have lived through a similar experience gives that message of encouragement and hopefulness, both to immediate victims and to the watching world."

> *The victims-to-leaders principle.* Becoming a leader
> is the best way to rise above being a victim.

The students had seen for themselves that being in service to others can be a potent affirmation of one's self, as well as a path toward healing.

Guided by this hard-won wisdom, these young people stood ready to answer the call of the next school tragedy (which seemed, at the time, a near-certainty). Alongside their terrible memories, they added the ability to see images of the future they wanted and what they might *do* to bring it about.

The group filled a backpack to show us what their contribution could be. Matt pulled each item from the bag as he spoke.

"When it happens next," he told us, "we'll send a backpack filled with tissues for when they cry. With water because you get dehydrated when you cry. And with candy and Disney videos for when they begin to feel better and maybe can even laugh a little."

A few months later, they were called on to ship 100 backpacks to a school in Minnesota.

To this day, I'm still deeply moved when I remember the time I spent with these young people.

Yet I hesitated telling you this story. There is something sacred about their experience that belongs to them. In the end, I wanted to honor their courage and wisdom by giving you the chance to learn from them, as I did. They showed me, in an especially poignant way, what can happen when the common discourse of despair is interrupted in order to draw attention to the life and hope contained in a situation.

They also taught me one more time that there are many ways to tell the story of an experience that we didn't want to have. Even in our most difficult times, we can choose a narrative that gives us a new and stronger sense of our capabilities.

That sense might well include such human characteristics as courage, tenacity, resilience, and faith, which can exist only if life holds challenges. "When the heart grieves over what it has lost, the spirit rejoices over what it has left," the Sufi say. In my own life, I can see my mother's early death as a time of sadness and loss. From a different (perhaps more distant) vantage point, I'm able to see how that experience contributed to my sense of myself as strong and independent. Both accounts of that event can be called true, yet they shape my self-identity in very different ways.

Working with the great kids from Jonesboro, Columbine, and Paducah also strengthened my conviction that people, including so-called "victims," know a good deal more about their lives — and about what can be — than the "experts" who are trying to help them. Sure, there had been psychologists at each of the schools who did what they could to help the kids, to reassure them and teach them how to cope. But the students didn't tell stories about receiving professional assistance; they told stories about how they had been there for each other.

There comes a time to trust ourselves and the wisdom that can be drawn from our own best experiences.

BUT I'M JUST
TRYING TO HELP

"If you have come to help me, you are wasting your time," says Australian aboriginal elder Lilla Watson. "If you have come because your liberation is bound up with mine, then let us work together."

Although helping has long been seen as a virtue, it hides a risky subtext. To be sure, the world is a much better place because people care about the well-being of others. But the form we give to our caring makes a big difference. In particular, I've come to believe that the framework of "helping" tends to separate people.

Eduardo Galeano, a Uruguayan journalist, puts it this way: "I don't believe in charity. I believe in solidarity. Charity is vertical, so it's humiliating. It goes from the top to the bottom. Solidarity is horizontal. It respects the other and learns from the other. I have a lot to learn from other people."

It's a bit of a paradox: Our caring acts can inadvertently strengthen and solidify another's self-image as "needy."

Moreover, when they've become permanent beneficiaries of our good deeds, individuals, organizations, even entire societies may begin to take on a permanent victim mentality. We can act with the best of intentions and yet foster a lasting sense of deficiency and dependency, what psychologist Martin Seligman has termed "learned helplessness."

Street children in Africa and students in America have proven to me there's a better way to act on our caring: walk the path with others, side by side in kinship.

The Crippled Children's Society of Southern California marked its belief in this posture when it renamed itself AbilityFirst. The name symbolized confidence in the children it served. It proclaimed to the kids and their families what they were made of. And it reminded all those engaged in the agency's work that they were *with* these capable kids and their families, rather than stooping to help the pitiful.

"The greatest good you can do for another," wrote Benjamin Disraeli, "is not just to share your riches, but to reveal to them their own."

How might things be different if we always sent to others the message "I believe in you," rather than "I pity you so"?

THE PARADOXICAL
THEORY OF CHANGE

And how might things be different if we sent that message, "I believe in you," rather than "You need to change"?

Most social causes strive to change people: to persuade them to adopt a certain viewpoint, get involved in their communities, stop polluting, start exercising, take time to enjoy music, stay in school.

Contrary to the popular notion of resistance to change, I've found that people are more open to change than one might expect, even eager for it. What we object to is *being* changed; understandably, I'd say. Like the framework of helping, the notion of changing another person carries hidden messages: "I have the right answers and you don't, so you'd better listen up. After all, I know what's good for you. (In fact, I'm better than you.)"

Well! With that music playing in the background, it's little surprise that we see people resist our efforts to change them, however honorable and well-intentioned we believe ourselves to be.

Perhaps paradoxically, change happens more easily when we begin to genuinely see and honor the assets and unique perspectives that others have to offer. In other words, when we support their strengths instead of trying to fix what we think are their "defects."

This insight harkens back to the work of Abraham Maslow, who was the first psychologist to study healthy people. He observed that healthy chickens are good choosers. For example, they naturally select the food that is best for them. Similarly, when people are supported, feeling full and strong, they are apt to see more choices and to move naturally toward health and growth.

It's also reinforced by recent findings about how the brain works.

Researchers have discovered that the brain reacts strongly when it senses something unexpected in the environment. These "error signals" come from the orbital frontal cortex, a part of the brain that is closely connected to the amygdala—the brain's fear circuits. When these structures are activated, they draw energy away from the areas of the brain that support higher intellectual functions.

Telling a person to change a habitual behavior triggers this built-in mechanism. The natural result is that the person becomes uncomfortable, emotional, and impulsive. So the research says that a person who is "resistant" to change, or "defensive" about criticism, simply has a normally functioning human brain.

What if we stopped using up so much of our energy trying to change people?

Might it even be useful to go so far as to learn to accept (or even appreciate) the very behaviors we object to, which may have a value that we simply have yet to understand? For example, we might learn to see what is commonly called "resistance" as a person's way to express their desire to be heard, to be taken seriously as someone who matters, someone who cares. Besides, it's easy, I've found, to experience a choice for a person that they don't experience for themselves; that is, to see options for them that may be outside their awareness.

Taking this idea a step farther, those "undesirable" behaviors may even be a gift to us. "I have learnt silence from the talkative, toleration from the intolerant, and kindness from the unkind; yet strange, I am ungrateful to these teachers," wrote Kahlil Gibran. In the end, loving kindness toward those teachers (a tenet, of course, of Buddhism, Islam, Judaism, Christianity, and other faiths) is bound to leave some for ourselves as well—just as in virtually every faith and culture the Golden Rule urges us toward an ethic of reciprocity.

BUT I STILL WANT TO KNOW
HOW I CAN IMPROVE

Even more useful than trying to change people is to un-
cover what is already there. As Picasso said, "I don't develop. I am." So often, there is something latent, ready to
be revealed when the conditions are right, perhaps just
waiting to be noticed.

Nearly two decades ago, someone revealed a capacity
in me that I was certain wasn't there. And it changed my
world.

You've seen the surveys of what people fear most. Public speaking is always right at the top of the list. For someone like me whose preferred style is introversion, it can
be downright terrifying. I'll always remember the first
speech I gave as a teenager — head down, eyes glued to
my index cards, so scared I was sure I had the flu.

In the years that followed, my work often called me to
present in front of groups. I continued to write out every
word of my talks and stayed close to the security of my
script. Once in a while, I'd make a little eye contact with
the audience, but not so much that I'd lose my place and,
heaven forbid, have to wing it.

In the late 1980s I decided I wanted to improve my performance. So I went out looking for a speaking coach and
found an exceptional one in John Jones of San Diego.

John flew to Calgary, where I was scheduled to give
my next seminar. At dinner the night before the event, I
put myself at his mercy. "John, I'm really looking forward
to hearing your criticism," I said, flinging my arms wide

to show him how open I was. "I'm ready. That's what I want."

John smiled. "Oh, I won't have any criticism for you, son. I'll only tell you what you're doing well."

I thought to myself, "What? If I'm going to get better, I've gotta know what I'm doing wrong." But it was a bit late to try to negotiate his approach.

Sure enough, at the first break the next day, John had no criticism. In fact, all he gave me was a list of the skills he saw, and a suggestion that I practice them when I went back in front of the group. I found myself feeling pretty good. After all, here was an expert giving me evidence of how capable I was. Maybe there was something to John's mysterious ways.

A little later in the day, John offered one suggestion that intrigued me. "Did you notice, Jim, that people paid even more attention that time you stepped away from your notes? Would you want to try that again?"

Take a close look at what he said. He pointed out a moment when I was doing something he knew to be effective. (I'm sure I was clinging tightly to the podium, so believe me, it would've been a very brief moment. But a small glimpse was all it took.) I now had a place to stand in confidence. That made it possible for me to take the next step, and the next. A series of small wins set up a trajectory.

As you can imagine, that day was a turning point for me, thanks to John.

Fast forward eight years. I'm standing in a living room in Santa Monica, speaking with the board of Conservation International. Among those in the room is the actor

Harrison Ford. As we're about to take a break, he says to the group, "You know you can ask me to do anything for this cause, just don't ask me to speak extemporaneously like Jim Lord just did. Give me a script, and I'm fine." If heroic Harrison Ford had only known where I'd come from.

Today, I still feel butterflies in my stomach as I head to the front of a room. And then I remind myself that Frank Sinatra, surely one of the world's most able performers, said he knew those butterflies were a sign that his show would go well.

It occurs to me that this story may sound like it's about how smart I am. Actually, it's an example of changing the world—my world—to get something I wanted, to find myself capable of something I thought impossible.

And it's a story of how such a breakthrough came about because people showed me what I already had in me.

WHAT
DO WE *WANT?*

Sometimes the default modes—solving problems, meeting needs, changing people—make it hard to see what is already there that provides a path to the world we want. Let's take this idea to the organizational level.

A few years ago, a major U.S. telephone company called in a large consulting firm. Some 80 percent of the company's female employees had reported experiencing sexual harassment on the job. The company wanted the consultants to solve the problem.

The consultants brought in lawyers and trainers, and organized a series of workshops. It wasn't long before employees stopped showing up to the sessions. It became more difficult for them to talk about the subject. Reports of harassment actually increased.

Puzzled, one of the consultants called David Cooper-rider, who we met earlier. Right away, David asked, "Well, what do you want?"

"We want sexual harassment to stop."

"No," said David. "What do you *want?*"

Again came the same answer.

David repeated his question a third time.

The exasperated consultant sputtered, "Don't you get it? Don't you know what sexual harassment is? We want it to stop."

"How about you talk it over with the folks there and call me back when you know what you want," said David.

The next day his phone rang again. "OK, we've got it," said the consultant. "We want effective cross-gender working relationships."

"Good," David responded. "Now we have a place to begin."

He then introduced the consultant to a systematic way of focusing on what people want to move toward, rather than what they don't want. Employees were asked to identify and describe high-quality working relationships between men and women at the company. David thought they might find a couple dozen stories.

They found hundreds. And reports of sexual harassment began to decline.

The change came about because people became clear about what they wanted, and then intentionally sought to see more of it already in their midst. They began paying attention to times when men and women worked well together, instead of dwelling on the times when those relationships caused distress.

In sharp contrast, the initial round of anti-harassment training—a bureaucratic dressing-down replete with cautionary tales and dreary lists of "don'ts"—had left the employees feeling they'd fallen short. The implicit message from management was that employees were untrustworthy and that elaborate rules were required to keep them from betraying their colleagues.

Thanks to David's intervention, they learned that they weren't really a bunch of jerks. They saw themselves differently. Their sense of competency and confidence grew when they saw they were already capable of having high-quality working relationships.

When we take time to notice it, we may find we already have more of what we want than we thought.

WHAT IS YOUR WORK
REALLY ABOUT?

Clarity about what we want can also lead us to rethink the very nature of the social causes we support.

Imagine this scene: A researcher watches as a five-year-old girl draws a picture of her extended family. The girl grabs bright-colored crayons and carefully draws her smiling parents, brother, and sister in the middle of the paper. Then she reaches for dark gray to sketch her grandparents, smaller and off to the side.

Theresa Bertram got wind of this research and thought about what it meant to her: As young as five, we've begun to hold images of diminishing as we grow older.

Theresa is executive director of the Cathedral Foundation, a service arm of the Episcopal Diocese of Jacksonville, Florida. The Foundation had earned a national reputation for its services to senior citizens, including retirement communities and Meals on Wheels.

Still, Theresa wasn't satisfied.

"We'd built our services based on what was best for seniors, as we saw it," says Theresa. "We were responding to external factors—medical problems, isolation, lack of engagement. And we were focusing on programs for which funding was available."

"This was under the banner of restoring independence," Theresa continues. "But it occurred to me that when we deliver meals to people at home, or care for them in retirement communities, we might actually create or perpetuate isolation and dependence. We might inadvertently preempt a different response from their families, their neighborhoods, or the community."

Theresa began to wonder what could happen if the Foundation stopped focusing solely on meeting what many consider the needs of seniors: meals and custodial care. She began to reflect on whether the Foundation might make an even more significant contribution to society.

Theresa engaged Kathy Wells, a local consultant who had studied the processes upon which this book is based, to conduct an assessment of the Foundation. (Kathy, you may recall, was asking questions in Jacksonville about civic cooperation at the time her colleague was looking for heartburn issues.) When she first started to work with Kathy, Theresa saw the assessment as the first step in a conventional strategic planning process.

"But I was struck by the transformational language in Kathy's report," says Theresa. "She talked about tapping our latent energy and dreaming about possibilities, rather than beginning with a plan."

The following month, the board decided to start on the path Kathy had shown them: finding the Foundation's future—its best future—using the methods of appreciative inquiry. In a memo to board members, chairman John Sefton called it "a bold step that requires vision and faith in ourselves."

It was an especially bold move because the inquiry would not focus on the Cathedral Foundation and its programs, how much money it could raise, or even on the needs of the Jacksonville community. Instead, it would explore the larger question of aging in American society.

Cathedral Foundation would convene a conversation about the best that aging could be.

"An interview protocol was designed to evoke the best experiences of older people—and younger people in the presence of their elders—and to find out what conditions made those experiences possible," says Theresa. "What we find will let us develop a vision of our organization's future, based on how we can create the best possible circumstances for the people we serve," Theresa continues. "In the end, what we learn from this process will make it possible to reframe the whole discussion about aging, and begin to create a new set of social expectations."

SEVEN

RECLAIM
THE POWER TO
CHANGE THE WORLD

WORK FROM
WHO WE ARE

Some years ago, I spoke at a dinner for Esperanza ("hope"), an agency that provides medical care in Latin America.

I asked the group: "Given the work that each of you does with Esperanza to benefit people far away, could you tell us about when you first became aware of the world around you?" A great question, or so I thought.

I wanted them to think about how they had acted because of *the kind of people they are*, but they took the more usual response. They focused on *how compelling the needs were*. And so we heard story after story about what's wrong with the world. (This was early in my work with these ideas; otherwise, I would have called a time-out and reframed the question.)

That's the way people usually frame their actions on behalf of the common good: "I did it because the need was so compelling."

But could it be that our actions actually say something much more significant about *us?* The situations may seem important, but we might also think of circumstances as simply a catalyst, an opportunity to express who we are as human beings.

As we'll see, it takes some doing to shift the focus so that people can see what they bring to the table and how their actions add meaning to their lives. Yet that awareness provides the footing on which we stand when we make our greatest contributions.

IS THE FUTURE
WITHIN EMILY?

"When our daughter was 15, she got a part time job. Her first paycheck came to $98."

That's how Debbie MacDougall began telling me what happened one afternoon in their small town near Vancouver. Debbie had driven Emily to the bank to deposit that first check in her brand new savings account.

When Emily got to the counter, she said to the teller, "I'd like to keep $50 in cash."

Debbie interrupted her daughter to give her a lecture on the importance of saving.

Emily listened quietly to Debbie's parental advice. Then she said, "Mom, the $50 is for the Christmas Hamper project at school." Emily was in charge of the school's initiative for the nearby women's shelter.

"I think it's important to set an example for other students," said Emily. "The project is worth half my paycheck, don't you think?"

"Tears welled up in my eyes before I could even blink," Debbie told me. "I was astounded. The teller gave me a look I'll never forget."

A few months after hearing this story, I met Emily in the course of my work with the school. She seemed like any other student. Who would have guessed that the scene at the bank would have unfolded as it did?

That's the power of this story: that such a universal desire to make things better, to make a difference, to set an example, was there all along.

When we take time to notice, remember, and tell others about moments such as these, they begin to take up more space in our minds and hearts—and in the systems in which we live. We transcend the downward draw of deficit discourse and crowd out doubt and despair. These images and stories begin to reshape how we view other people and what we believe might be possible for society.

That's plenty, but what might be possible if we assumed from the start that the desire to contribute, to do good, is already there, instead of feeling we have to struggle to convince people to do the best and right thing?

After all, it took no prompting for Emily and her classmates, in their senior year, to raise enough money to start a school in Ecuador. Inspired, the next senior class built one in Sierra Leone, and the next in Kenya.

OUR CONTRIBUTORY SPIRIT
SHOWS UP EVERYWHERE

Although "contribution" is usually associated with the social sector, I'd suggest that the built-in contributory spirit extends far beyond that traditional realm of good works.

Two colleagues, one from Hong Kong and the other from Germany, first brought this idea to my awareness. (It's significant to me that this thinking came from outside the United States.)

They persuaded me to develop the idea that the contributory spirit offers a way to organize our thinking about what happens in corporations, small businesses, government, families, communities. (Might we even think of paying taxes as an expression of our shared desire to act for collective benefit?)

In all of these settings, people want to be a part of something beyond themselves. Contribution is an important way, subtle or silent as it may be, that people say "I'm here, I matter." Wherever they are, people want to make a difference.

It seems to me that the social sector has a lot to teach about activating that built-in contributory spirit throughout all of society. We'll return to this idea in the next chapter.

THE HIGH ART
OF DENIAL

However strong the desire to contribute might be, there's an equally strong tendency to deny that our efforts have made any difference.

Let me tell you why I'd say that. I grew up on Lake Erie, swimming every day all summer long. Then one summer the perch began to float belly-up around me. Today, I'm deeply grateful to the people who took initiative and restored the lake — and to everyone who is a steward of the wonders of this planet.

A few years ago, I wanted to express that gratitude when I was on a panel that included Peter Warshall, then editor of *Whole Earth* magazine. During the public forum,

I tried to thank him for his work on behalf of endangered species. Peter would accept none of my appreciation. He could see only the failures, the species that have been lost, and the magnitude and urgency of the work that still lay ahead. "No," he said, "extinction is forever, and every day the loss is incredible. We cannot rest."

I stood my ground. "Well, even if you close your ears, Peter, I am grateful to you for what you've done."

It still surprises me: Hundreds of interviews we've conducted have confirmed that people give their all to make the world a better place, and then refuse to admit that they've had any effect. Even when it's clear that a person has made contributions of great consequence, they'll deny their power and influence.

"I haven't done much," said a board member of two national environmental groups, during an interview about his life of contribution. He had invested decades of personal leadership—and hundreds of thousands of dollars—in that cause and others important to him. Still he discounted his part and denied what he had accomplished.

Entire social movements can even come to dismiss their contributions to society.

Pam and I worked on the first chapters of this book in a small town near Minneapolis. One afternoon, we took a break to get some exercise. On our way to a new community center, we were talking about some grumbling she'd been hearing from her colleagues in the environmental movement: "People just don't care about the environment. Environmentalism is dead."

Could it be true that decades of dedicated effort to raise awareness had gone for naught?

We walked into the community center. Etched into glass at the top of a wall, in letters ten inches high, were eight words representing the community values that were commemorated in the building. Right in the middle: "environmentalism."

Just a few months after that experience, we marveled that people all over the world were paying to watch a film of a former U.S. vice president's slide-show lecture on global warming.

All around us are signals that we have indeed been effective in advancing our highest ideals. Why do we seem so determined to deny that we've had any influence? It's really something.

Could it be that we're just trying to seem humble? After all, we've spent our lives being taught to perfect our skills of self-deprecation. Perhaps we habitually move our accomplishments into the "taken for granted" column, as we do with so many good things in all areas of our lives. Maybe whatever we've achieved is simply eclipsed by our admirable desire to get on to the tasks that remain.

I certainly admire a refusal to rest on one's laurels. But when we notice our successes and acknowledge the part we played in bringing them about, we take a crucial step toward even more effective social action.

SUCCESS IS MORE THAN
AVOIDING MISTAKES

In these pages, I've suggested we can find ourselves a more confident, inspiring, and hopeful vantage point. Many people assume that it's somewhere up in the clouds, and are surprised to learn that in fact it's on solid ground.

A growing body of research in management and in the social and behavioral sciences provides strong support for learning from success instead of only seeking to correct deficiencies. That might be tough to buy, so let's work with it for a moment.

Sports psychology gives some especially vivid illustrations. In one typical experiment, people learning to bowl were divided into two groups: One group was only shown videotapes of their successes. The other half was shown only their mistakes.

The first group, the ones who focused on what they did well, improved twice as much as the second group.

In all kinds of athletics, such methods are becoming a vital part of training. Jack Nicklaus, widely considered the greatest golfer of all time, tells us how important it is to hold a mental picture of success. A successful shot is much more likely when a golfer is told to "hit the ball down the middle of the fairway," rather than "don't hit the ball into the trees."

What's going on here? Why in the world would it matter how we phrase what seems on the surface to be the exactly same goal?

Only the picture of what we want — the picture of success — gives us an image that we can hold in our minds and use to guide our actions. It's easy to envision a golf ball soaring in a high arc straight down the middle of the fairway.

But what does "don't hit the ball into the trees" look like? The only clear picture associated with the phrase has an unintended effect: Research has shown that the mind tends to ignore the "not." We're left with only the image of *hit the ball into the trees*, the opposite of what we want to happen.

Still, our social conventions, those habitual patterns of thought and language that we construct in our everyday conversations, draw us toward a continuing cascade of correcting mistakes. So I yell to the kids at the pool "Don't run!" even though I know full well that "Walk!" would be a better choice. The words pop out of my mouth before I think.

The same patterns play out in organizations, also without thought. We seek to identify problems, fix mistakes, learn from failure — and we institutionalize those habits in structures and practices that become unquestioned routines. I try not to forget (I mean, I try to remember) how ingrained it is to see the world this way. It goes all the way back to childhood, when we were mostly told what not to do.

And these common practices work, or at least they work well enough for most of us, most of the time. Remember that the bowlers who saw only their mistakes *did* improve. But those who saw their successes improved much more.

If our goal is to continue to advance incrementally, in small steps, then the traditional deficit approach may be equal to the task. After all, we've had lots of practice, we've become very good at it, and it has served us well enough.

On the other hand, if we want to dramatically advance our organizations and the causes we care about, we might find ourselves asking: What's the *best* way to inspire, mobilize, and sustain the desire that people have built in?

LOCATING THE ENERGY
FOR THE FUTURE

Ever hand a piece of your writing to someone to get their reaction or approval?

I did that a lot as I was beginning my career. Usually, the person would go straight to the gap between what they saw and what they thought it could be. (As H.G. Wells said, "There is no passion in the world greater than the passion to alter someone else's draft.")

Now, it's useful that people can see a gap. It shows they have high aspirations. But focusing *only* on the gap drains our energy.

Decades ago, the president of Indiana Bell showed me another way of working, when I gave him a piece of copy to review for Butler University. Instead of plunging into critique, he told me what he liked about the piece. "It's simply amazing," he said. "I don't understand how you people do this." I met the man for an hour, and would have rewritten the copy all night long for him.

That same kind of approach can energize and encourage people in all sorts of situations.

Charley Whiton, when he was a county commissioner in Wyoming, told me about a meeting that had him squirming in his chair. His fellow commissioners were lamenting what they had just learned: seven out of ten high school students in their part of the state had tried drugs. The hand wringing was intense. Many people had chosen to live in the community because they thought it would have fewer of these "big-city problems."

Now, Charley is a friend of Anne Nickerson, who we met earlier. Remember how she came to realize that others shared her hopes for her community, so she decided to start speaking up with confidence? Charley had participated in a community-building initiative, together with Anne and others in their town, which had sharpened their ability to use the ideas we've been working with in this book. He was the only commissioner who had that experience.

Charley told me that in the meeting of the county commission, the framework he had learned "cried out to be applied."

"So when I spoke," he continued, "I asked what turned out to be a surprising question: 'What about the other three? You could just feel the tension melt away, as they began to think about working from the power of the three, rather than the problem of the seven."

WHERE DO WE
GET THE NERVE?

There's a lot more at work here that makes this posture so powerful.

We've seen that when we focus on what we have going for us, we fortify our confidence and raise our spirits. We enliven ourselves. In contrast, a deficit orientation can be deadening. Even more, it often leads to fear and defensiveness, two of the greatest inhibitors to human enterprise.

That sure fits with my own experience. I know that when I'm feeling threatened, I want to hunker down and shut out the world. And when I feel good about myself — capable and competent, supported and fortified — I'm much more likely to be open-minded, try new things, even take initiative. Probably you've had similar experiences.

Research into brain chemistry has shown that these reactions happen at a cellular level, far outside our conscious control. It's widely known that anxiety and fear activate the most primitive parts of our brains, triggering the fight-or-flight response that shuts down rational thought processes. In fear mode, instinctive reactions are often all we can muster. After all, it's hard to be creative or thoughtful when your brain is busy fighting off a tiger.

When we feel more secure, we activate the parts of our brains responsible for logical thinking. We become physically able to think more clearly. What's more, we're more likely to experience positive affect, which has been linked to increases in creativity, learning capacity (especially when learning something new), decision making and judgment, pro-social behavior, and emotional intelligence.

(We're also healthier in general: Positive connections with others have been shown to promote physical health. This is very important to me, as I've seen, and felt in myself, what we commonly call burnout, so prevalent among those most dedicated to the common good.)

When we pay attention to success and let ourselves feel good about what we've accomplished, we take full advantage of what's known about the way our brains work.

KNOWING WE
HAVE THE POWER

Learning from our successes has yet another significant result: It increases our belief in our self-efficacy. When we see vivid proof that our actions have led to the results we wanted, however few and far between the instances may be, we're compelled to admit (perhaps reluctantly) that we are indeed capable of influencing our surroundings and making a difference in the world.

Seeing oneself as more effective and powerful can advance every dimension of an individual's life. And when a group of people shares a strong sense of efficacy, they'll see more choices available to them, set their sights higher, put more effort into reaching their goals, remain resilient in the face of circumstances, and increase their likelihood of success.

There's been a good bit of research done on self-efficacy, and it holds some surprises. For starters, it up-ends the conventional wisdom that it's important to be realistic about your abilities, and that holding an inflated view of your capacities is bound to get you into trouble.

Instead, the research shows that the people who overestimate their own capabilities are the very ones who make the best use of their potential.

This shakes up yet another popular notion: That a sense of accomplishment, or even just plain feeling good about yourself, is a character flaw (or worse, sinful). It means you're prideful, smug, "full of yourself." And it leads to laziness and complacency.

So when we do feel powerful or accomplished, even if momentarily, we may doubt ourselves, or chalk it up to dumb luck. We may even feel the "imposter complex," especially when others give us more credit than we think we're due, and rush to give all the credit to someone else, or to providence.

All of these feelings are understandable. But in fact, cultivating a strong sense of self-efficacy is extremely valuable. Doing so lets people see more options for action, more ways to exercise their talents, more avenues for self-expression and contribution. It may seem counterintuitive, but seeing the full extent of what we've achieved makes us more ambitious, not less.

The bottom line for those who want to make a difference in the world is this: People who hold "unrealistically" rosy opinions of their abilities also tend to make the greatest contributions to society. What is often dismissed as self-deception is actually very functional. Indeed, it's essential if we're to aspire to anything beyond the routine.

What I find especially fascinating is that self-efficacy is best developed by actual experiences of successes, times when we show ourselves that we're competent and capable in having influence on the world around us. It's also developed by seeing others—especially others who are like us—having such experiences.

Simply being *told* that we are capable builds a sense of potency to some extent, but these *actual experiences* are much more powerful.

So if we want to increase a person's belief in their own efficacy, we'll make a little progress by telling them how great they are.

A far more effective approach would be to offer them opportunities to live and relive their successes and the successes of others—to study, savor, and learn from those best experiences. When this practice moves beyond a person or two into a larger group, it can magnify its power and invigorate whole systems.

Perhaps most important, we gain faith that the future is open to our influence.

That's more significant than it may seem at first blush. Recall Frederick Polak's observation that a culture's rise or fall depends on of its guiding image of the future: A vital image of the future means the culture is flourishing. A bleak image and the culture's prospects are dimmed.

Polak also observed that promising images of the future emerge most strongly when people share a strong sense of what he called "influence-optimism"—a belief that the future can be influenced and that we are capable of influencing it. (You'll recognize this as a close cousin to the notion of self-efficacy.)

For those of us who work to bring about social change, a stance of collective efficacy can make history.

THE REVOLUTION
HAS ALREADY BEGUN

So that's one way to give an account of the world: tell stories that paint a picture of a world that works, a world where there are at least islands of achievement, a fundamentally encouraging and hopeful view in which individuals and their actions matter. More commonly told is another set of stories that leave us with very different images: failed states, collapse, disaster, impending doom.

If Frederick Polak was right, our choice to tell one set of stories or another is much more than a simple judgment about which set is more "accurate" or "reality-based." It's a choice that can actually influence what will happen and how things will turn out. It just might be the most important choice we can make if we care about the future of people and the planet.

Rather than hold the world as dismal and oppressive, we can allow promising stories to crowd out the others. One narrative that I find especially exhilarating is the story of how powerful we have become because so many of us are freer than ever before. I hope you'll indulge me for a few moments and perhaps see what this account suggests to you.

Human freedom is greater now than at any other point in history. The progress has been swift. Little more than 200 years ago, "the bulk of mankind, over 95 percent, were miserable slaves or tyrants," according to economic historian Stanley Engerman.

Another measure: At the beginning of the 20th century, not one nation could be described as democratic, if judged by the standard of universal free elections. Today, 121 of 192 nations can be called democracies by the same standard.

Freedom has taken giant steps with the spread of literacy and education, as well as the dramatic improvements in human health that have given many of us much longer lives (a development so profound that we'll return to it in the final pages). And in just the last decade, the Internet has changed the distribution of power and enhanced human freedom in ways we have yet to fully grasp.

Individuals are freer than ever before to effect social change by acting on their personal passions, increasingly trusting themselves rather than solely trusting authority.

We can already see this freedom taking shape as a groundswell of voluntary action. Here's the tip of the iceberg from just one sector: A global network of volunteers develops open-source software (including most of the software that runs the World Wide Web) and gives it away for free, putting increasingly powerful communications tools into the hands of billions of people. Politics, journalism, and publishing are being reshaped as amateur bloggers and self-published authors take advantage of these new means of influencing the world, while repressive governments find it increasingly difficult to keep a lid on free speech.

Such leaps have astounding and exciting potential for human liberation. Even more important, it seems to me, the developments are themselves proof of the human desire and capacity to achieve, to grow, to collaborate, to create, and to take charge of our lives. If we have more freedom, more options, and more opportunities than ever before, it is because we've made a series of choices.

Together we have created the new beliefs and ideals, new institutions and infrastructure that support both our individual potentials and the evolution of society as a whole.

EIGHT

WHAT CAN HAPPEN WHEN WE BELIEVE IN SOMETHING?

CAN HISTORY BE MADE
IN A BOARD MEETING?

The greatness of our organizations is vital to the future. After all, we live in organizations. By working together in organizations, we can change the headlines in the newspapers, the lives of our fellow human beings, and even the course of history.

But when we walk down the hall to a meeting, how many of us think about the historic significance of our work on behalf of the cause we serve? It's easy to get so wrapped up in the details (the day-to-day "how") that we lose sight of the high aspirations for which an organization stands (the enduring "why").

Yet it's the "why" that both defines and fuels the greatness of social sector and civic initiatives. After all, the "why" is the reason we create these causes in the first place, as vehicles for reaching our aspirations for society. And the "why" is the reason we continue to pour in our time, energy, and money.

If we fill ourselves with this sense of historic import, what do we make of the growing pressure on social sector organizations to become more "business-like"? And what do we make of the closely related insistence that we look solely to "outcomes" and rely exclusively on numerical measures to assess an organization's effectiveness?

As Robert F. Kennedy Jr. said of the gross domestic product, we may be measuring "everything ... except that which makes life worthwhile."

Might we choose to go for breathtaking, extraordinary, world-changing action, rather than just making the numbers?

And might the distinctive features of the social sector, its mission-driven and value-laden nature, be reason to pause before embracing standard business methods?

DO "NON-PROFITS"
HAVE SOMETHING TO TEACH?

Dick Boysen, executive director of the Guilds' School and Neuromuscular Center in Spokane, Washington, called me on the phone one day.

"We're just finishing up our strategic planning, and you know how I try to stay away from 'stinkin' thinking,'" he tells me. "But I've got to admit it: the staff is feeling beaten up. All they can see are the gaps between where we are and where we want to be—the places where they're falling short."

I could easily imagine what Dick was going through: An organization decides to project what might be on its horizon. It's practically an article of faith that this is accomplished through something called "strategic planning," one of many practices the social sector has borrowed from the business world in recent years. So the organization hires a consultant and does a strategic plan, assuming that's the best way to get to their next level of success (or at least stave off failure).

Why does the outcome so often disappoint?

Well, to begin with, strategic planning has had mixed results even in the business sector. A global study of 1,854 large corporations found that over the span of a decade, seven out of eight fell short of achieving profitable growth (that is, returning more than the cost of capital). Robert Kaplan and David Norton reported in *Harvard Business Review* that 90% of the companies studied had gone through the exercise of creating detailed strategic plans.

Even more to the point: Standard strategic planning practices, rooted in business models of human behavior, simply are not designed to tap into the contributory spirit and high ideals that are especially visible in the social sector. Martin Luther King Jr. did not say, "I have a strategic plan." He shouted, "I have a *dream!*" and created a crusade.

If our work is born of passion, conviction, and taking a stand for what we believe in, then why overlook that energy in favor of the more superficial and mundane?

To my mind, what happened at the Guilds' School is an example of the common struggle to squeeze high ideals into the confines of flow charts and spreadsheets. The school's staff are among the most talented, creative people I've ever met. They're passionately dedicated to the kids they serve, so they take great pride in doing their best. In fact, they bring to their jobs a devotion—a sense of mission—that businesspeople often only wish they could develop in employees.

So how could a seemingly routine strategic plan have shattered their confidence in themselves?

We've seen that focusing on strengths gives people the confidence to notch up both their ambitions and the belief that they can deliver on those aspirations. Instead of such a life-affirming approach, typical strategic planning gives equal time to internal weaknesses and external threats. Given our collective and individual tendency to overvalue the negative, people can quickly become overwhelmed and demoralized by wallowing in what they lack.

For the school's staff, people who find deep personal significance in their work and hold high aspirations for all, the experience was devastating. They saw the plan as proof of how badly they'd fallen short of their most cherished ideals. They saw only the weaknesses that had been identified, the gap between *what was* and *what could be.* Believing they'd been portrayed as inadequate, they felt shame in front of their CEO and their board.

I've seen this happen time and again, especially in organizations with the highest hopes and most capable staffs.

And more than a decade ago, it dawned on me that we may have had it backwards: Instead of feeling embarrassed and deficient, or compelled to play catch-up to the business world, the social sector actually has a lot to teach businesses about what makes people tick. After all, how many businesses get people to show up as volunteers and work for free (and even pay for the privilege by contributing money) or to work as staff for much less money than they might be paid elsewhere?

Today this insight is beginning to spread. Jim Collins, author of the best-selling business book *Good to Great,* wrote in a recent monograph on the social sector: "Social sector organizations increasingly look to business for leadership models and talent, yet I suspect we will find more true leadership in the social sectors than the business sector."

The leadership role of the social sector is also evidenced by the spread of idealism in the business world. A growing number of businesspeople are taking up the banner of social responsibility and seek to imbue their work with more meaning and significance. They are putting into practice one of the great lessons of the social sector: the power that comes from standing for what we believe in and acting on our ideals.

INSPIRED
TO THE CORE

"You might begin at the beginning," I offered to Dick when we resumed our conversation about the Guilds' School. "You could start by looking for what the school has going for it, and wallow in that for a while."

Dick called a time-out on the strategic plan, then gathered his staff and board together for a carefully considered purpose: To tell stories of their best moments at the school, in order to discover what had been at the heart of their success as an organization.

Believing in one another. That's what they found at the heart of the school and their work, at the center of the many assets and strengths they uncovered. Of course, you might expect people at a school would believe in kids. But at the Guilds' School, that core is so vital, so pulsating, that it overflows into relationships with everyone who is involved with the school: staff, siblings, parents, board members. Everyone. (Even me, an outsider.)

The realization of this identity, this DNA of the school, flipped their state of mind from deficit and defeat to genuine, grounded power.

They also had gained more *information:* the stories provided evidence from their own experiences, proof that showed them what they were capable of and what mattered most to them. This made it possible to envision a successful future for the school that was both ambitious and well-founded.

Out of this strength grew many new ambitions, including a bold idea for an international conference that the school soon developed and still hosts today. The conference lifted "believing in one another" to include their colleagues from afar, indeed their entire profession. In the course of a single year, this small school, barely known in the state but deserving of much wider influence, became an international leader in advancing its field.

"We reached firmer ground," Dick told me later. "We had more clarity about who we are and what we bring to the table. That made all the difference in raising our sights. When all we could see were our failings, there was just no way to imagine we could succeed, much less make a big leap."

The school had also moved beyond strategic planning in another important way. People experienced with planning often acknowledge that the tricky part comes when it's time to actually execute the plan. Even when implementation gets off to a good start, resolve may falter from time to time.

When the Guilds' School chose to begin at the beginning and see what they had going for them, they built the energy for sustained action right into the process. More precisely, they found the energy and idealism they already had in them, waiting to be released.

Once again, we see the importance of the simultaneity principle—the idea that the seeds of change are embedded in the first question we ask. We've already seen other examples: the company that dealt with sexual harassment by inquiring into high-quality cross-gender working relationships, the organization that asked for stories of success even though it had just laid off staff, the two consultants in Jacksonville who got very different results by asking very different kinds of questions.

Whenever we set out to move a group or a cause forward, we have a choice: We can build confidence and energy by fortifying the health and vitality that's already there. Or we can show people their deficiencies and expect that will motivate them. You already know where I'd place my bet.

So what happens when we follow the example of the Guilds' School and build on the greatest strengths of the social sector: passion, conviction, taking a stand for what we believe in, idealism, contributory spirit?

Well, we find that we can organize in ways that express our beliefs and aspirations (rather than compromise our values to get the results we seek). We can create the world we want by starting where we live: in our organizations.

And rather than treat social sector organizations as "wannabe" businesses, surely a deficit approach if ever

I've seen one, we can strengthen their distinctive strengths and watch them thrive.

BUT IS THE DREAM
FEASIBLE?

"When we were starting out, it seemed like some huge new obstacle appeared every day. No kidding, every day," Debbie MacDougall told me in one of our many conversations about the founding of Southridge School near Vancouver. (You met Debbie earlier, when we learned about the contributory spirit from her daughter Emily.)

This independent school was founded without a big gift, without a wealthy patron, without a feasibility study.

"If we'd begun by analyzing the 'feasibility' of founding a new school, we probably would've stopped dead in our tracks," Debbie says. "We wanted the school, so we just kept finding ways to bring it to life."

Gary Hamel and C.K. Prahalad, leading thinkers on business strategy, echo Debbie's thoughts from their experience in business: "Where fit is achieved (between resources and ambitions) by simply paring down ambitions, there will be no spur for such ingenuity and much ... strategic potential will remain dormant. Tests of realism and feasibility must not be prematurely applied."

If that's true in business, it may be even more true in the social sector. After all, the resources available in this realm are not a "given" that we can calculate in advance. We're working with the built-in desire to contribute, to invest ourselves in society, to make a difference. We can strengthen that desire by giving people a chance to bring to the surface hopes that they long to see realized.

So why let our initial hunches (or fears) about feasibility limit our imagination, vision, and enterprise?

Instead of trimming their dreams to fit their seemingly limited resources, Southridge's founders trusted themselves. They focused on what they had going for them and what they wanted. They tapped into their own deep stores of will and desire. And they stretched their aspirations far beyond their apparent resources.

When Southridge admitted its first students, it was $18 million in debt. I like to call it a "reverse endowment." Some might call it risky, perhaps even foolhardy. But stretching toward the dream has worked. While steadily paying down its debt, Southridge has managed to keep its tuition among the most competitive in the province, and its academic rank among the very highest. In fact, as early as its seventh year, it was named the best school academically in British Columbia.

Am I saying we can simply forget about being "realistic" and completely ignore the obstacles in our way, or the possibility of abject failure?

Well, I'm sure tempted.

Instead I'll suggest that we can let questions of feasibility take a back seat for a while. Doing so gives you room to make absolutely sure that you've taken into account all the things you have going for you: every single one of the useful circumstances that surround you, the entire inventory of the assets and strengths of your organization and its people. And that you've fully appreciated them, thereby increasing their value.

(We'll see in the next few pages that the confidence resulting from such a stance can attract audacious investments, as people come to see how your organization advances the kind of world they want.)

At the same time, you can begin to let go of the notion that your organization's potential for success is limited by forces in the world, community, or the field in which you operate. Again, Jim Collins observes that he encountered an interesting dynamic as he began to study the social sector, where "people often obsess on systemic constraints," when they could move forward with what they *can* do to advance the kind of world they want.

If you do find circumstances that seem daunting, or perhaps even opposed to what you want in the world, you might see what happens when you ignore them. They just may turn out to be less important than you thought.

THE LITTLE TOWN THAT COULD

Many, perhaps most, causes and social sector organizations are held back by their sense that they don't know how to raise money and advance their situation, or by a general distaste for the whole endeavor of "fund raising."

But after decades in the field, I'm confident that the raising of money is in fact the very *best* place to find the heart of civic action, or any kind of leadership on behalf of the whole. I'd like to share with you a classic story along these lines, from the early years of my work in the field.

Shelby, Ohio, 1976. Population 10,000.

The board was ready to throw in the towel. For an entire year, they'd been planning and organizing to raise $800,000 to build the first phase of a YMCA community center. The first dollar was yet to be raised and they'd begun to despair. For weeks on end, they'd been having the same conversation, reinforcing over and over their belief that they didn't have it in them to succeed.

"This town is too small."

"It's too much money.

"Nobody cares."

Board member Bob Lederer, then 29 and president of a local packaging company, saw more in the town and its people (perhaps as Churchill had seen in his country?). He grew increasingly impatient with the board's downward spiral.

One evening at a meeting in a church basement, he stood up and said he'd heard enough.

"Tell those who would doubt that we can do it, Yes, we can!"

Bob later backed up his words with a significant financial commitment by his company, a tangible expression of his faith in this enterprise and in the town's future. Bob's example changed the agreed-upon reality and others began to step up. Soon the town was buzzing with excitement about the new community center. A banner reading "Yes, we can!" was raised over Main Street.

More companies joined in making leadership pledges. A group of factory workers came to the campaign office late one night after a meeting at their union hall. They set their own example by each donating an amount equal to the cost of a bottle a beer a day for three years, to shock their company's hesitant leaders into a major commitment.

One day, a waitress in Sid's Coffee Shop, who said she was a single mother working hard just to make ends meet, leaned over the counter to ask me whether she could make a small contribution (as if she doubted her money was good enough).

Within a year, the campaign had met its goal. The banner that flew over Main Street was changed to read, "Yes, we are!" The town celebrated with a parade. And the board decided to keep going to raise the long-range goal, which had earlier seemed like a far-off dream: a total of $1.4 million.

The campaign drew nationwide attention. A UPI reporter and photographer came to Shelby. The story of the "Little Town That Could" ran on front pages across the country on July 4 of the bicentennial year, and inspired a nation to show its support.

One child in California wrote on a piece of notebook paper, "I think this is a great idea," taped two quarters to an index card, and put it in the mail. A woman from West Virginia sent a five dollar bill "from my social security check." Imagine what these heartfelt expressions meant to the people of Shelby.

Once the $1.4 million had been raised, the banner was changed again, this time to read "Yes, we did—thanks to you!" And they marked the occasion with another parade.

At the banquet held to celebrate the conclusion of the campaign, my boss, John Rhodes, and I were invited to toast the town's achievement. So grateful was I to have been a part of the town's accomplishment that I could barely get out the words: "You've done it. You said you wanted to build what you wanted, how you wanted it, where you wanted it. And the success is all the sweeter, thanks to the early doubts."

Even today, I'm moved to remember how that small town did something they were sure was impossible. For me, it meant something far beyond doing my job, far beyond the raising of money, far beyond the building of the community center.

I had seen people coming to know their personal and collective ability to shape the world as they wanted it to be.

I had seen the profound leadership-by-example that can be contained in a single courageous statement, a single defining investment.

NINE

BRINGING FORTH
THE BEST

WHY DO PEOPLE
INVEST THEMSELVES IN SOCIETY?

That early experience in Shelby was the beginning of my own picture of what I want the world to look like. As the "Yes we did!" banner was stretched across Main Street, I saw it all around me: People striding down the street with little smiles on their faces, aware of what they'd accomplished, feeling their oats. It showed only slightly, but it was there: People with renewed confidence in their abilities and a stronger sense of self-efficacy.

After all, I knew it was the strengthening of this identity that both led to the financial success of Shelby's campaign and grew out of their achievement.

Still, an important question remains: *Why* do people invest themselves in society? If we want to draw even more people to contribute their time and money to the common good, it would be useful to understand why people do these things.

I've been wondering about this for a long time. At age 22, I had just joined Ketchum Inc. as its youngest consultant. My first day on the job, I naively asked, "Why do people volunteer? Why do they give money?"

I'm still fascinated by these questions. But I've given up on trying to answer them in any definitive way.

The president of a global relief organization once asked me, "We know a lot about why people give through direct mail. But what about major donors—why do they give?"

I replied, "I don't know." (Imagine that!)

The executive vice president, who had taken me into the president's office, squirmed in his seat. "Jim, just this morning you were saying …." He tried again, "I remember reading in your book …."

"Yes, I'm aware of all of that," I answered, "but still I don't *know*."

Of course, there are plenty of ways to explain the origins of giving. While theologians look to divine guidance, evolutionary biologists puzzle over the survival value of seemingly unselfish acts. Psychologists talk about "cognitive dissonance," the desire to unite our behavior with our values. Theories abound.

Such attempts at universal explanations are intriguing. But I'm much more interested in learning from the lived experience of an individual human being. Rather than believe that I have people in general (or any person in particular) figured out, I want to stay curious and in wonder. Standing shoulder to shoulder with another, I want to have a genuine exploration of the meaning contained in that person's actions.

As a bonus, my experience has been that this approach energizes the will and initiative of the individual, and thus holds the greatest potential to activate contributions that are even more significant (both in meaning to the individual and in amount).

This learning benefits more than me. For starters, staying curious gives the person a chance to develop *their* understanding of the dynamics at work in themselves and their contributions. That personal understanding is one of the most powerful pieces of knowledge they can bring with them into the organizations or causes in which they are most engaged.

Here's a simple example from the way staff at the University of Michigan prepared for a $3 billion campaign. In the middle of a flip chart, we wrote the name of a gentleman who had made one of the largest commitments to the university. Then the small group offered factors and conditions that they believed had influenced that person's decision to invest. They included even something as seemingly small as a casual comment made by the receptionist.

As we began to discover the lively interplay between all parts of the system, we created our own theory of contribution, a theory distinctive to the university's history, culture, and community, and to the particular individual. Such a specific, complex, nuanced understanding stands in sharp contrast to the more usual view that contribution results from simple, generic cause-and-effect mechanisms.

Afterward, the key staff leader said that with all they knew and all of the success they had had, this was the first time she had understood deeply why someone would give to the university.

A close look at the experience of just one person can yield more home-truths than all the surveys and feasibility studies we can conduct and all the quantitative research we can study. The answers are found in the systemic swirl of forces and conditions inside and around the person and those closest to him.

(Notice I said closest to "him," rather than to the university. And notice that he gave the money, rather than the staff raising it. Sometimes it's a good idea to think of our favorite institution as something other than the center of the universe.)

I've had the good fortune to work with other universities and groups that seek to invite their philanthropic partners (the people who are more often called "donors") to raise *their own* sights by taking part in such an inquiry.

More often, insiders feel the heat generated by "needs" and push for quick results. So they issue requests for funds on a schedule dictated by internally defined necessity, rather than by the individual's growing sense of significance and self-efficacy. Lost completely is the far greater "oomph" that would have come from allowing the individual's own volition to emerge.

If you want to know how to raise money, I have a book for you: this one. Really. Take another look through this book with that question on your mind. After all, this book is about how people tend to behave when their contributory selves are present.

MONEY AS
MORAL LEADERSHIP

As we saw in Shelby, an exemplary financial commitment—one that is both meaningful to the individual and significant relative to their financial means—can set the pace for an entire community. Such a commitment serves to encourage others by example, rather than by advice. That was just as true for the factory workers and the

waitress as it was for such community leaders as Bob Lederer.

What can happen when people take stock of what their
investments have meant to them as individuals, and even
perhaps acknowledge the moral leadership they have
shown?

Barney Saunders, a Harvard alum, was vice chair of
the largest privately-held company in the world. Kathy
Wells and I met up with Barney in St. Paul, Minnesota,
where he had just become chair of the board of Hamline
University. (We last encountered Kathy some pages ago,
working with the Cathedral Foundation in Jacksonville.)
The university was in the early stages of preparing for a
capital campaign, and Kathy and I were there to work
with them in laying the groundwork.

Kathy interviewed Barney, in the spirit of this book,
about his experiences as a contributor. Because the interview was on behalf of a university, she also asked him
about his experiences with learning. She was curious to
find out what might be at the heart of his deep connection with the university's mission and work, and what his
highest hopes were for society.

We all know such questions are rare in the field of
"fundraising," which tends to be more focused on the programs and "needs" of an organization than on the experiences, hopes, and dreams of the individual.

After the interview Barney was scratching his head.
"Something happened here, but I don't know what it
was."

After reflecting on the experience through several talks
with the university's vice president, he concluded: "Har-

vard has asked me, they've asked me many times—but always for money. Neither Harvard nor any other organization has ever asked what's important to me. Hamline will get all of my money, and Harvard will get no more."

Barney went on to make a contribution of such financial and moral significance that it set the pace for the largest capital campaign by far in the university's history. So much momentum was created that the university increased the goal. At last count, the campaign had gone beyond even that mark.

And I saw on Barney's face that same little smile I'd seen on the streets of Shelby.

When something so transformative happens for a person, it also shifts how they think about raising money. Barney saw that it was he who had received a gift: the opportunity to reflect on the meaning of his contributions—and even on the meaning of his life.

"This is how I want to treat others," he said. "All trustees should be interviewed as I was, not for what more they can do for the university, but as a gift to them for what they've already done."

Barney expanded my understanding of the importance of focusing on meaning—the individual's dreams for themselves and for society—and lifting up confidence and self-efficacy. Such actions activate the built-in desire to invest oneself in society, and do so in a way consistent with our aspirations for the world.

In the end, money follows meaning.

UNLEASHING
THE DESIRE TO INVEST

If meaning and self-efficacy are key to people investing money in an organization or cause, is it any different when the people who work as staff invest their time, energy, and creativity?

Take the annual ritual of employee performance reviews, where these ideas of meaning and volition are apt to be set aside, even in the social sector. The usual approach is to "get down to business," correct deficiencies, and fit the individual into the organization's priorities.

"You've done such great work this year, Bob. But here are three areas where I'd like to see you improve (for your own good). And by the way, I've redesigned your job."

Why do we act surprised when Bob seems less than grateful for our direction and input? Or when he loses his "game" because his individual talents and desires have been ignored, any passion thwarted, and all he hears is the criticism, however carefully and "constructively" it's offered? (Remember that any "resistance" he may feel is just a sign that he has a normal human brain.)

Are you ready to entertain the idea that there might be better ways to accomplish our ends?

Weary of the usual ritual, one manager who's worked with the ideas in this book experimented with a radical notion: unconditional positive regard in the workplace.

That's right, Linda did performance reviews that contained not one word of criticism, even though there were aspects of some staff's behavior that she would have preferred to be different. She decided to trust herself and set aside the HR department's forms and procedures, with their deficit-based assumptions and numerical rankings.

She saw herself in service to her staff, as in Robert Greenleaf's notion of "servant leadership." She set out to do whatever she could to provide the conditions conducive to her staff's aspirations for themselves and for the world.

When Linda met with each person for their annual review, she asked them to tell stories of their high points on the job during the past year, times when they had been especially energized and alive. (These might have been states of "flow," in the parlance of psychologist Mihaly Csikszentmihalyi.) Together, the two of them explored what had made those best moments possible, what gave life to that particular individual and their work. They even talked about what was at the heart of their dedication to the organization and the cause it serves.

Linda concluded each session by asking the person to describe what success would look like for them in their work during the coming years. Because they had taken the time to look back, relive their best moments, and connect with what mattered most to them, they set far higher aspirations for themselves than Linda ever would have dared to suggest (or even imagined).

Each person painted a picture of success that was drawn from the colors of their unique talents, on a canvas of their highest hopes for themselves and for the world around them.

Lest you think such an approach is a license for individuals to run amok, pursuing pet projects to the detriment of the organization's agenda, I'd suggest the opposite is more often the case. Once people truly have been seen and heard as distinctive human beings (which demands of us that we bring our own authenticity), and have articulated for themselves the meaning of their work (which demands of us that we have articulated our own meaning), they are more apt to contribute fully to the success of the organization and its cause.

And guess what? In the months after these conversations, Linda saw less of the behaviors a more conventional manager would have sought to correct during performance reviews.

Now, you may think Linda must be a softy. And she is indeed a tender, caring soul. But she's also a devotee of extreme sports and an intrepid mountain-climber. And during this same staff review process she fired someone who was less dedicated to the cause than Linda expects of her colleagues.

This is not about being soft or hard on people. It's about applying what is known about human behavior to invite them to make their highest contributions, and doing so in the most effective, straightforward way. When we set aside conventional assumptions and learn about what actually makes people tick, we have to ask whether criticism can ever be "constructive."

This notion can be extended to other relationships in our organizations. Take a scene that's more commonplace than we'd like to think: a board meeting where the chair says to the staff person, "I'm going to set this aggressive numerical goal so you'll lie awake at night worrying about how to meet it."

It doesn't seem to occur to the chair that the staff person cares so deeply about the cause that she *already* loses sleep as she wonders how to make the organization even more successful.

We can all admire this board chair's desire, even his impatience, to urge the staff to new heights. I'm sure he would tell us that he brings to the table an important sense of rigor and focus. Still, the negation and criticism, the sheer insult, inherent in such efforts at imposing "discipline" can demoralize even the most dedicated of staff. (Besides, as we saw at Guilds' School, people can do plenty of self-criticism on their own, as they let their habitual tapes play.)

Brave and enlightened leaders in the social sector have infinite opportunities to set up the conditions that deepen the personal commitment of people that is so central to success. Rather than try to "crack the whip" and "make it happen," they can give these matters a bit of time and some sustained attention, and allow the built-in dedication to come to the surface and flourish. Naturally.

WHAT WOULD
SUCCESS LOOK LIKE?

It may strike you as unusual, even a bit strange, to see staff evaluations and philanthropy (or "fund raising") treated in such close proximity. After all, those are usually considered entirely different tasks, even different professions.

But I've found it useful to think of both as examples of an unspoken aim at the very heart of the social sector: to lift up the most noble qualities in human beings. Indeed, if you think about it, might that even sum up the highest purpose of the sector, a purpose that we could intentionally carry into the ways we work together?

When we make room for conversations about what we have going for us, what kind of world we want, and why our aspirations matter so much to us, we also make room for bold answers. We make it possible for individuals to see that the world they want actually might be possible and that they are capable of making a difference in bringing that about.

Then, *of their own volition,* they will set their sights higher. And then, freely and gladly, they will act—inspired acts grounded in their own convictions.

No one asked Barney Saunders to make such a sacrificial financial commitment. Nor did Linda ask her staff to set audacious goals. They made those choices because someone had carefully and mindfully invited their idealistic selves to come out of the closet.

As we've seen, these same ideas can be applied to reveal the boldness and energy latent in an entire group of people. Recall how the staff and board of the Guild's School looked back to the best of their past and present, to find the "stuff" of which they were made. Once they had taken stock of their assets and discovered their core ("belief in each other"), they were poised to ask themselves what their next level of success could look like. As we've seen, they gained the energy and confidence it took to dream more boldly and to turn that dream into action.

Yet it's common to skip or short-circuit this step, in all aspects of organizational and civic life.

What could be possible if we systematically allowed the greatness in people to come forward, and let their built-in contributory spirit be even more visible?

IS IT UP TO
SOMEONE ELSE?

Several years ago, Elinor Magnuson, a community leader and former Junior League president in Spokane, Washington, asked me to work with her on a day-long event that would bring together 150 community leaders. The gathering would take place one week after a bitterly contested mayoral election that had divided the community.

Elinor and I ran into one of the mayoral candidates on the street a few months before the occasion. She wanted both of the candidates to attend, so she told him about the idea. Of course, by the time of the event, one would be the victor and the other the vanquished.

The candidate said he would be there, win or lose. He said he liked the idea of an "envisioning meeting" and told us he thought some healing would be called for by then.

I thought to myself that I saw the day differently: as a forum for people to come together to find what they wanted their contribution to be to the community—perhaps even their greatest contribution. And I told him that.

The day would begin by listing all the community had going for it and each person's ambitions for the kind of world they wanted to live in. And then *each individual* would consider the specific contribution they wanted to make to foster that kind of society.

Why not come together to heal and to envision the future, as the mayoral candidate assumed we would? For starters, using "healing" as our framework focuses attention on illness and pathology.

More important, I've seen many people go through the exercise of creating a vision of the future of a community (or organization). And often the long-term results have disappointed them because the process left out the key ingredients: *individual* passion and commitment.

You've probably been at one of those meetings: People get together to talk about the future and it turns out they mostly want to brainstorm ideas for other people to carry out.

A few years before the Spokane event, I attended a large conference in Orlando, Florida, where some 3,000 people gathered to promote voluntary citizen action. The next day's newspaper quoted a participant who'd said it was a good meeting and he was looking forward to seeing what the *government* would do with their ideas. So strong was the default assumption—it's up to someone else—that neither the participant nor the reporter had caught on to what was supposed to have been the whole point of the conference.

In contrast, the design for the Spokane event grew from my belief that if people are going to aspire to something for the good of the whole, it's best if they begin with what *they* want to contribute. After all, ideas really come alive only when individuals commit to them.

Especially in the voluntary sector, how do we carry out a "good idea" that no one truly holds as their own?

BUY A TICKET, GEORGE

Many of us leave the action we desire in the hands of God, supernatural forces, pre-arranged destiny, the sweep of history, Mother Nature, or other forces apparently beyond the influence of individual human beings.

But even if we believe (as I do) that there are larger forces at work in the world, we can still lead our lives recognizing the power of the individual. Maybe the best way to handle such weighty matters is with a light-hearted fable.

A fellow named George prayed all day long one Saturday. The largest lottery drawing was to be held at 6 that evening. Every hour on the hour he prayed: "Dear God, let me win. Dear God, let me win." At a quarter to 6, he said his last prayer. "Dear God, please, please let me win. I'll do anything."

Suddenly he heard a deep voice speak to him from on high. "George, do me a favor. Meet me half way. Buy a ticket."

HIGHER GROUND

If we lift up an individual's dreams and ask what they want to do to bring those dreams alive, then the organization becomes a vehicle through which people can work to realize their hopes. Each person can ask some unusual questions: How does this organization fit into my life? How does it serve my aspirations for myself and for the world?

This is the spirit of the founding of an organization, isn't it? In the early days as a group emerges, the founders give shape to their personal dreams through the vehicle of the new organization. They work to bring into being the kind of world, or corner of the world, they want.

As time goes by, it's easy to lose that founding passion and unthinkingly adopt the opposite view: that individuals exist to serve the organization. Collective priorities start to dominate, often in the form of good ideas developed by a small group for other people to carry out. Those others (volunteers, donors, staff) are expected to fall in line and do as they're told.

Somewhere along the way, the flame of personal passion and voluntary action may start to flicker.

The ideas we've explored in these pages hold promise to keep the founding energy alive, even as an organization matures and new people join in.

How?

You already know: By letting people pull themselves into the future, fueled by their built-in desire to contribute in a distinctive way to the good of the whole. By fostering more passion than control, more personal fire than self-sacrifice.

And by focusing first on higher ground: the *world* each of us wants and the *cause* that can be a vehicle to advance that desire.

That higher ground of individual desire, so clear in the beginning, can become fuzzy as the routines of organizational life limit the choices we see available. The early desire to change the world often turns into a more modest wish to balance the budget and keep the doors open, a minimalist survival mode that misses the larger "why." That's understandable, especially since it's become fashionable to adopt bottom-line business practices that sometimes discount the idealism and fervor that fuel the social sector's higher aspirations—and lives in people ready to do things.

When we move our attention back to the world we want, and to society as a whole, we rekindle that passion and enterprising spirit. When we lift ourselves up out of our daily routines, we bypass the organization's habits of talk and thought, the "it can never happen here" and "we don't have the resources" conversations. We gain more license to be creative, to dream boldly, and to act with more conviction.

Oddly enough, our "wishful thinking" at this larger scale can then begin to manifest itself in our day-to-day organizational lives.

I learned this through my experience with the Cathedral Foundation, the organization devoted to elders that we encountered earlier. You'll recall that the Foundation turned its attention to creating a new framework for aging in American society. The cornerstone of this effort is an interview protocol that elicits stories of personal experiences with older people, drawing forward the person's highest hopes for growing older.

In the early stages of this work, some of the Foundation's staff were interviewed. Each person had a meaningful, and most unusual, opportunity to consider the personal significance of the Foundation's work. They reflected on their experiences, their lives, their hopes and dreams for themselves and others.

Soon after these interviews, something completely unexpected happened: the Foundation was able to stop relying on temporary agencies to fill in its nursing schedules. This was a big deal, I learned, as such low absenteeism is simply unheard of in the field, and temporary nurses are very costly. This development had a measurable positive effect on the financial bottom line. And surely the quality of nursing care benefited from the increased continuity of staffing.

Here's the most surprising part: Only the central leaders, as far as middle managers, had been interviewed. No nurses had participated directly, yet they were feeling the effects of the changed atmosphere in their workplace.

Our ideals for the world, once given voice, naturally begin to sing more clearly in our everyday work.

BUT WHAT ABOUT
COMMON GROUND?

With this experience under my belt, I was even more convinced that a search for higher ground is powerful, especially when born of the experience and dreams of individuals.

How different this notion is from the prevailing assumption that finding *common ground* is the best way to move forward. The usual approach is to work as hard as we can to reach consensus, get everyone on the same page, and hammer out a plan, with incentives and measures to enforce accountability.

To be sure, the pursuit of common ground has honorable intentions. It is one way to get ourselves organized and ensure that we have some clarity about shared goals, what we're up to as a group, and who's going to do what. At least on the surface, it seems a reasonable way to stave off chaos and get something done.

But it's also a sure way to mute differences, individuality, and personal commitment—and to get deeds less inspired and less fulfilling than might have been.

What happens when we intentionally accentuate and heighten awareness of our individual differences, rather than rush to find what we have in common?

It may seem counterintuitive, but this may well be key if an organization is to reach its highest potential. Strategy guru Gary Hamel puts it this way: "New voices (i.e., new genetic material) must be brought into the strategy process. Diversity was a requirement for the development of life; so too is it a requirement for the emergence of new strategy."

Organizations that actively seek out and value a wide range of differences, far beyond merely "tolerating" diversity, will naturally become more alive, more vigorous, more creative. They'll be nourished as the living systems they are. So perhaps instead of trying to "get everyone on board" with the dominant voice, we want to legitimize and amplify the marginalized and muted, and gain the power inherent in mixing together people of different degrees of positional power and status.

That might sound like a recipe for conflict, but the dynamic is actually much more subtle. Recall the paradoxical theory of change: When we appreciate what's different about someone, rather than trying to change them to be like everyone else, they're more relaxed, secure, and open. We're more apt to contribute our best when we're first respected for who we are. And the effects ripple outward, as we also become more able to appreciate others.

What happens when we activate as much difference as possible?

Here's a taste of what could be: Imagine you're involved with a human service agency in your community. You walk into a large hall and see the whole system in the room: people who deliver services, make budget decisions, provide philanthropic investment, and even those who benefit from the agency's services. Vendors, elected officials, "competitors," partners. The receptionist, the CEO, the middle manager, the trustee, maybe even the janitor. They all sit together, deeply engaged in conversation, and provide the widest possible range of vivid colors from which to paint a picture of the world they want.

Consider this in contrast to the more usual exchanges of information and decision-making through a series of isolated, sequential meetings among homogeneous groups.

Using these typical practices, more often than not we end up with muddled colors that we can all agree to, but that no one really wants enough to pour their heart and soul into. We try to get after-the-fact "buy-in" from constituency groups, when we could have facilitated the passionate commitment of individuals from the start.

We may bring our better selves to common ground, but we will bring our best selves to higher ground.

TEN

YOUR UNEXPECTED
PERSONAL POWER

HOW OFTEN HAS THE MONARCH LED A REVOLUTION?

The traditional view is that "change must start at the top." So we wait for our leaders to act, even though we can see what is called for and we know what we want to happen. It's worth remembering that historically it has been the dispossessed—from Gandhi to Mandela, from the American patriots to the Polish shipbuilders—who have brought about the greatest social changes.

As Vaclav Havel, first president of the Czech Republic, once put it, "Small, futile moral actions can bring down an empire." Indeed, one of the sparks that set off the peaceful 1989 revolution in Czechoslovakia was the jailing of a rock band over freedom of expression.

Certainly there are forces operating, tailwinds that give lift to our cause. Still, the precipitating moment often takes the efforts of only a small group of people, as Margaret Mead observed.

Sometimes that small group is children. New seeds and cultivation methods had been around for many years in early 20th-century America, but farmers weren't open to using them until an enterprising extension agent from the government suggested to the children of farmers that they ask their parents for a small corner of a field to experiment. "How did you ever get such corn yields from that same land?" the farmer asked his children. "I can ask the county agent who taught us to stop by," the kids replied. And in that creative idea, which in time became the 4-H Clubs, an agricultural revolution was born.

A century later, in a very different world, Russell Simmons speaks to youth, to those his own age (49), and to
all of us when he says our personal commitments count
for more than we think. "If you see yourself as powerless,
you are," says Simmons, "if you see yourself as powerful,
you are. If you see the world as a great place, it is; if you
see the world as a place that sucks where no one has any
opportunities, it is."

As a teenager, Simmons was a drug dealer. He's now a
successful record producer (sometimes called the godfa-
ther of hip-hop).

He says he's inspired to act when he sees young people
taking the future into their own hands, "when I see them
registering to vote, when I see them changing laws and
cheering about the laws, when I see people telling me they
are inspired to be an activist themselves because they see
what can be done collectively, when I see them becoming
leaders on their own."

"Voting is a statement to yourself that you see yourself
as powerful and able to make the world better," says Simmons of the effect that our actions can have on our confidence in our own power.

YOU ACTUALLY MEAN
ME?

"Little ol' me? You're saying *I* can change the world — or even just my small corner of it?"

Well, yes. After all, each of us has already made a difference.

Raising a child to be "a good person."

Bringing home a paycheck, especially doing work that holds little intrinsic meaning.

Voting.

Saying a kind word to a stranger.

These are contributions. They can even be downright heroic.

Each and every one of us has the capacity to make the most fundamental contribution of all: showing up as ourselves, authentically, with the richness of our life experiences.

A few years ago, I met a woman who was in her 80s. Her beloved husband had died years before, but the memory was fresh. As we spoke, once in a while she'd glance at a large portrait of him that graced the wall of her living room.

"Right after Bob died, a friend came over and sat next to me," she told me. "She put her hand gently on my knee and began to speak. In my stupor, some of the words sounded familiar. And then it came to me: She was trying to counsel me, using techniques I knew she'd learned one summer in the church basement. I had to ask her to leave."

"Then another friend came to visit," she continued. "She was younger than I, but her husband had died a couple of years earlier. She just sat with me, saying nothing."

A long pause as she remembered that day.

"That was what the doctor ordered. She was my proof that I could survive this. Her very being was evidence."

It may seem a small thing, comforting a grieving friend. What does it have to do with the high ideals and historic matters we've been talking about? Being present for family, friends, and neighbors usually isn't counted as "voluntarism" or being "in service." Surely it doesn't qualify as changing the world.

But when you really stop and think about it, don't those seemingly small moments contribute to creating the kind of world you want to live in?

On the societal scale, these acts of personal connection are direct human-to-human services of such magnitude that would cost governments billions to provide (if they even could).

Taken together with the more obvious forms of voluntary deeds and philanthropy, such individual initiative creates an invisible economy so large that futurist Alvin Toffler has described it as the hidden half of the world's wealth.

"I am done with great things and big plans, great institutions and big successes," wrote William James more than a century ago. "I am for those tiny, invisible loving human forces that work from individual to individual, creeping through the crannies of the world like so many rootlets, or like the capillary oozing of water."

We can still aspire to great things and make big plans. I'm only asking that we also pause just long enough to notice what we usually call small things — the everyday ways each of us shapes our own corner of the world. A poster from some kids, two widows sharing silence, a conversation with a friend, a remark to a colleague, a question in a meeting.

"Small things" influence the world more than we know.

YOUR GREATEST CONTRIBUTION

Whether you're sitting with one other person or leading a country, your greatest asset is simply your presence: who you are, where you stand, how you show up. As Gandhi suggested, when you pay attention to the quality of your presence, you begin to create the world you want.

Your presence becomes even more powerful when you choose to see the world from a higher perspective, to stand for the lure of your ideals, and to show your confidence in the future and your belief in other people.

I've seen the power of that kind of presence time and again.

"When I'm on campus, the problems seem so real. There's always someone going on and on about some urgent need or looming crisis," Dan Loritz, vice president of Hamline University, said to me one day. "But when I step off campus, I can see the university as the beacon of hope that it is. And *that's* the reality I stand in when I meet with people of the community—and try to bring back to campus."

You might expect someone like Dan, who works with exemplary philanthropic leaders like Barney Saunders, to keep in his breast pocket a list of its top ten funding needs, or maybe his top ten "prospects." Instead, he carries with him a list of everything Hamline has going for it, a letter-sized sheet of paper completely covered in the smallest handwriting you can imagine.

Dan looks at that paper every day. He knows it takes some doing to stay true to such a confident, aspiring, and idealistic posture.

I learned 30 years ago how easy it is to let that stance slip away, when I hired a writer to develop a case for support for the Pittsburgh Zoo. I gave Steve my first book, *Philanthropy and Marketing*, which proclaimed that "nonprofits" would be more effective if they focused (yes, here we go again) on ideals and assets rather than problems and needs. So I thought he'd return from his visit to the zoo with a donor-centric, society-focused case that would excite investment. Much to my surprise, he wrote a "case of complaints."

"Did you read the book, Steve?"

"Sure, I read it," he replied. "And then I got together with the director and he told me about the conditions at the zoo. He took me around and showed me how bad it was. The cages were old. The growth of the hippos was stunted because of the small quarters. Bears were pacing in cramped cages. I *had* to write about the needs."

As I've said before, the downward pull to which Steve succumbed is little more than a habit, toward which we all drift at times, myself included.

If we've chosen a different stance toward the groups and causes we care about, we can find our bearings again. When we invest our money and talent, we can adjust our framework so we send a message that reinforces others' courage. We can let people know we believe in them. We can point them toward what they *have*, their resources and capacities. We can give them even more confidence in their ability to make a difference, instead of perpetuating their self-image as "needy," deficient, and even powerless.

When we take this higher road, we show true leadership, moral leadership and faith in the future, rather than merely giving away money and time to meet "needs."

Could this message and our presence be a contribution greater than our money or time?

All of this may be in your hands far more than you might have thought. For I've noticed something about you: You've been reading this book. Really, I'm serious. I find it hard to imagine that anyone would stay with this book if they'd given up on society, or on their ability to have at least some influence on the future. You could have put this book down at any time, so I have to believe that something about you is reflected here.

I have more than a hunch that your idealism has been supported, reinforced, and expanded as you've read these pages. A rather clear and simple proposition is offered: It may be up to people like us, you and me, to turn the world's attention from needs to resources, from problems

to possibilities, and from despair to confidence, and to elevate our species to its highest potentials.

MIGHT WE
SHIFT OUR GAZE?

If the stories we tell are so central to how things turn out,
where do we look for stories to encourage us, stories to
provide the energy for a future of promise?

Here's one way of thinking about this question. Imagine looking through a camera, with the lens tightly focused on one spot in the foreground. Everything else is
fuzzy and indistinct. You then refocus the lens to a place
in the background, and bring that into focus. And what
was clear before is now hazy.

Stories of needs or images of problems may be in the
foreground, but we can willfully shift our attention to
something that is useful and encouraging in the background. When we draw it forward, its arrival crowds out
whatever had been the focus of our attention, and pushes
it into the diffuse background.

If one part of life offers little to sustain us, we might
shift our gaze to another aspect: to an individual, our
neighborhood, nature, God's love, faith in humanity, the
causes in which we believe, the miracle of the universe,
the marvel of discoveries past and future. There is always
a level of system, whether tinier or greater, that can inspire us.

The place we choose to stand, the stories we choose to tell, and the power we choose to claim have a heart so simple, so obvious that it's apt to elude us.

CAN YOU SEE A GLIMPSE
OF THE WORLD YOU WANT?

Barely a week after 9/11, a group came together for a workshop at the University of British Columbia. After we'd puzzled over some of the unconventional ideas and improbable questions you've read about in this book, I asked them: So what is it that we're working toward? After all is said and done, what kind of a world is it that we want? What kind of world do *you* want? Can you express it in a single word, or maybe two?

I'd asked these questions of groups many times before. That afternoon it was different. I spoke with a lump in my throat. The words came out softly, in my deepest voice.

The first person to answer said she wanted a "safe" world. Heads nodded. We could all relate to that wish. In fact, I have a hunch that on that particular day, most would have called safety an urgent "need."

I wrote "safe" at the very top of the large sheet of paper on the wall.

Only seconds passed before Virginia Henderson offered another view. "I think it's a different world than safe," she said. "I think that's past. It's a confident world I want."

In that moment, Virginia shifted our attention. Before she spoke, we had become focused on our despair, our fear, our hunger for security, and the apparently insoluble problem of terrorism. Under the circumstances, it seemed unthinkable to speak of anything else. Virginia's words brought our inner resources into view, and opened the possibility that we might face the future with courage and strength.

I wrote "confident" next to "safe." We worked with other responses for a few minutes more. Then, as we looked at all of the assets we had written on that same long sheet of paper, at the workshop's outset a few days before, I posed another question that I always ask: Look to the words at the top of the sheet, those to which we aspire. Can we see here and now any evidence of the kind of world we want—any sign that at least some of what we want is already here?

The group had gravitated toward the notion of a "confident" world, so I picked up on that and added, "any evidence that you can see of a confident world?"

Silence. All of us, eyes moist, turned to look at Virginia, who had flown half-way around the world from Australia.

Scott Russell Sanders writes
of a backpack trip with his teenage son …

The day, our first full one in Rocky Mountain National Park, had started out well. I woke at first light, soothed by the roar of a river foaming along one edge of the campground, and looked out from our tent to find half a dozen elk, all cows and calves, grazing so close by that I could see the gleam of their teeth. …

Up to that point, and for several hours more, the day was equally unblemished. Jesse slept on while I sipped coffee and studied maps and soaked in the early light. We made our plans over breakfast without squabbling. I felt buoyant as we hiked along Cow Creek toward the waterfall. We talked easily the whole way, joking and teasing, more like good friends than like father and son. Yet even as we sat at the base of the falls, our shoulders touching, the mist of Bridal Veil cooling our skin, we remained father and son, locked in a struggle that I could only partly understand.

For the previous year or so, no matter how long our spells of serenity, Jesse and I had kept falling into quarrels … I had proposed this trip to the mountains in hopes of discovering the source of that strife. Of course I knew that teenage sons and their fathers always fight, yet I sensed there was a deeper grievance between us, beyond the usual vexations. Jesse was troubled by more than a desire to run his own life, and I was troubled by more than the pain of letting him go.

The peace between us held until we turned back from the waterfall and began discussing where to camp the following night. Jesse wanted to push on up to Thunder Lake, near 11,000 feet, and pitch our tent on snow. I wanted to stop a thousand feet lower and sleep on dry dirt. ...

He glared around at me, "You're the one who's spoiling it, you and your hang-ups. You always ruin everything." With that he swung his face away and lengthened his stride and rushed on ahead. ...

My quarrel with Jesse changed nothing about the Rockies, but changed everything in my experience of the place. What had seemed glorious and vibrant to me when we set out that morning now seemed bleak and bare. It was as though anger had drilled a hole in the world and leached the color away.

I was still simmering when I caught up with Jesse at the trailhead. ...

I could bear the silence no longer. "So what are my hang-ups?" I demanded. "How do I ruin everything?"

"You don't want to know," he said.

"I want to know. What is it about me that grates on you?"

I do not pretend to recall the exact words we hurled at one another after my challenge, but I remember the tone and thurst of them, and here is how they have stayed with me:

"You wouldn't understand," he said.

"Try me."

He cut a look at me, shrugged, then stared back through the windshield. "You're just so out of touch."

"With what?"

"With my whole world. You hate everything that's fun. You hate television and movies and video games. You hate my music."

"I like some of your music. I just don't like it loud."

"You hate advertising," he said, quickly rolling now. "You hate billboards, lotteries, developers, logging companies, and big corporations. You hate snowmobiles and jet-skis. You hate malls and fashions and cars."

"You're still on my case because I won't buy a Jeep?" I said, harking back to another old argument.

"Forget Jeeps. You look at any car, and all you think is pollution, traffic, roadside crap. You say fast food's poisoning our bodies and TV's poisoning our minds. You think the Internet is just another scam for selling stuff. You think business is a conspiracy to rape the Earth."

"None of that bothers you?"

"Of course it does. But that's the world. That's where we've got to live. It's not going to go away just because you don't approve. What's the good of spitting on it?"

"I don't spit on it. I grieve over it."

He was still for a moment, then resumed quietly. "What's the good of grieving if you can't change anything?"

"Who says you can't change anything?"

"You do. Maybe not with your mouth, but with your eyes." Jesse rubbed his own eyes, and the words came out muffled through his cupped palms. "Your view of things is totally dark. It bums me out. You make me feel the planet's dying, and people are to blame, and nothing can be done about it. There's no room for hope. Maybe you can get along without hope, but I can't. I've got a lot of living still to do. I have to believe there's a way we can get out of this mess. Otherwise, what's the point? Why study, why work, why do anything if it's all going to hell?"

That sounded unfair to me, a caricature of my views, and I thought of many sharp replies; yet there was too much truth and too much hurt in what he said for me to fire back an answer. Had I really deprived my son of hope? Was this the deeper grievance, the source of our strife—that I had passed on to him, so young, my anguish over the world? Was this what lurked between us, driving us apart, the demon called despair?

"You're right," I finally told him. "Life's meaningless without hope. But I think you're wrong to say I've given up."

"It seems that way to me. As if you think we're doomed."

"No buddy, I don't think we're doomed. It's just that nearly everything I care about is under assault."

"See, that's what I mean. You're so worried about the fate of the Earth, you can't enjoy anything. We come to these mountains, and you bring the shadows with you. You've got me seeing nothing but darkness."

Stunned by the force of his words, I could not speak. If my gloom cast a shadow over the creation for my son, then I had failed him. What remedy could there be for such a betrayal?

...

Before leaving for Colorado, I had imagined that he would be able to meet the Rockies with clear eyes, with the freshness of his green age. So long as he was in my company, however, he would see the land through the weather of my moods. And if despair had so darkened my vision that I was casting a shadow over Jesse's world—even here among these magnificent mountains and tumultuous rivers—then I would have to change. I would have to learn to see differently. Since I could not forget the wounds to people and planet, could not unlearn the dismal numbers—of pollution and population and poverty—that foretold catastrophe, I would have to look harder for antidotes, for medicines, for sources of hope.

ELEVEN

THE REDISCOVERY
OF IDEALISM

RECLAIM OUR HISTORY
AND OUR GREATEST LEGACY

"In everyone's life, at some time, our inner fire goes out," wrote Albert Schweitzer. "It is then burst into flame by an encounter with another human being."

Perhaps you, like Scott Russell Saunders, have been so touched by a young person's idealism that you paused to look more closely at your own. So often, hope in the voice of a child rekindles the elders' ideals. That could be their gift, the child teaching the parent.

From a different vantage point, we can look back to be inspired by our own youthful idealism. For we have also held high hopes for ourselves and for society.

We can tell ourselves those seemingly naïve hopes have been dashed, and let ourselves feel disappointed and disillusioned. Or we can choose to see a different slice of reality: We have changed the world.

Some might say that of our parents' generation, indeed of every generation. But I know from personal experience that my own, the baby boomer generation, has indeed done the impossible.

What seems strange to me is that we've largely forgotten the role that we played. Recall for a moment the opening pages of this book and the story of the eradication of smallpox, the first time that a global threat was solved by human cooperation on a global scale.

Some people are aware, at least vaguely, of this bit of history. Less widely known is exactly *who* carried out the campaign. As a recent PBS special reported, "young idealists" were recruited for the task of delivering vaccine to every corner of the Earth.

Dr. D.A. Henderson, leader of the eradication effort, recalls that "a number of them had rather long hair. They certainly weren't individuals who were likely to show up and be well-received at an embassy cocktail party, but they worked tirelessly. They were real heroes." (At least one did get dressed up. Larry Brilliant, now head of the Google Foundation, lived in a Himalayan monastery during the 1960s. Then a guru told him to put on a three-piece suit and go to work with the leadership of the World Health Organization to eradicate smallpox.)

Thanks to the heroic efforts of many, including assorted hippies, freaks, and do-gooders, there has not been a single case of smallpox since 1977.

During the years of the smallpox campaign, the same generation of young idealists reshaped society in countless other ways. We changed social agreements about the status of women and the significance of skin color, stopped a war, drove presidents from office, took responsibility for the health of the planet. We showed that "power to the people" was more than a chant, it was a sign of things to come.

Today, we can see the results all around us. Yet, as I've said before, we usually take those changes for granted instead of noticing how profound they have been and remembering how they came about.

We have every right to believe in ourselves and in our ability to create the world we want.

MATURE
IDEALISM

"To be fair to you, I think it would be best if this were my last class." And so in 1970, the only male student dropped out of one of the first college courses in women's studies. He told a friend in the class, "my being there restricted the conversation. It's best if people feel free to speak. In a few months or a few years, perhaps I can bring something to the dialogue."

I was that young student, just returned from a tour of duty with the U.S. Navy. The society I'd re-entered seemed as foreign as the Asia I had left. My world had been shaken in the spring of that year when four students at Kent State, an hour from my home, were slain as they marched for peace.

What a time. Who knew what would come of it, whether our society would even survive the violence and chaos? It's easy to see now that we'd survive, but back then?

Anger, even hatred, provided much of the fuel for the social movements of those years. For me, that women's studies class was a lasting lesson in how we can get energy from seeing what's wrong and what we cannot, will not, let stand. Much has been accomplished working from that stance.

But in the decades since, I've come to believe that it's hard to sustain social change that springs solely from anger and a sense of injustice, because that kind of energy cannot sustain *us*.

When we stand in anger, we blame and overwhelm people, ourselves as well as others, and make it more difficult for any of us to see another way to be. We wear ourselves out, as our nervous system sets itself for the stress of a fight. Or we resign ourselves to defeat and withdraw from the fray.

The more daunting we describe the problems, the more wrong we paint society, the less confidence is available to bring about the world we want.

As we've seen in these pages, a better path has begun to emerge. We now have the ingredients of strategies for social action that are more humane, more enlightened, more spiritually evolved, and even more effective. Righteous indignation may have provided the first impetus to act, but the world is different today.

Black South Africans certainly taught us this and more when they put aside hatred and retribution after apartheid, in favor of forgiveness. I was deeply moved to learn from one South African woman how strongly that spirit of reconciliation is held.

When she was a child, she told me, her parents were in a car accident in a remote area outside of Johannesburg. The first ambulances that responded left the scene when they found out that her parents were black. By the time a "black ambulance" arrived, it was too late. Both of her parents were dead. Amazingly, she is able to see a glimmer of value in that terrible loss. For she now recognizes its role in who she is — a person for whom forgiveness defines her life. And so I knew she truly meant it when she said to me, "We were, and are, all in this together."

Today we can spend a lot less energy on agitation. We can turn our attention to sustaining ourselves and others, especially when we learn to see that people are "with us" more than we might have thought. When we choose such a creative and appreciative vantage point, we elevate the most precious aspects of what it means to be human, and allow the fire of our ideals to burn brighter than ever.

Could this more mature idealism become the greatest legacy of the baby-boomers to the next generation?

THE YOUTHFUL
FLAME

Idealism lives in virtually everyone. In some, it is an ember, awaiting the oxygen of inspiration. In others, it has been burning more brightly, often finding expressions very different from the youthful activism that I remember.

I think of Dick Boysen, the fellow we met earlier at the Guilds' School. Dick was a student at Berkeley in the late 1960s. His "hippie" idealism thrives in his work as CEO of the school, which serves children from birth to three years old who have developmental delays. Dick has wanted—and has worked to create—a world where the smallest among us are treated with the dignity they deserve, a world where they know they are believed in, and a world where ultimately all children will be treated by the same standards.

And I think of Lee Mercier, a trustee of the Cathedral Foundation who served in the Peace Corps forty years ago. That spirit lives today in his board service, as well as in his law practice, where he muses over how he can best

serve estate planning clients in choosing the philanthro-
pies they want to support.

(The very idea that we can expect our work-a-day
world to hold meaning and be authentic to who we are is
a new notion that arrived with the baby-boomer generation's coming of age.)

People like Lee and Dick who have been active in the
social sector, whether as staff or volunteers, have been
joined in their idealism by a growing number of others
who directly express their aspirations in the business
world. Unprecedented attention is being paid to corporate social responsibility, sustainability, and social entre-
preneurship, or simply humanizing the workplace. The
lines between the sectors have been blurring, as making
money is interwoven with contributing to society.

The world's largest corporate citizenship initiative, the
UN Global Compact, seeks to "unite the power of markets
with the strength of universal ideals," says former UN
Secretary-General Kofi Annan. In 2004, more than 400
leaders from business, labor and civil society gathered for
the Compact's first worldwide summit (facilitated by David Cooperrider using appreciative inquiry, as a project
of the emerging Center for Business as Agent of World
Benefit). Hundreds more were on a waiting list, hoping
to attend. In his opening remarks, Annan told those who
had secured a seat that "far more of you were determined
to attend than we anticipated in our wildest estimations."

One of the first to speak up during this working session
was Lord John Browne, CEO of BP.

Browne was the first oil company executive to acknowledge the role of human activities in global warming.

"Denial is the wrong response, but so too is despair," Browne has said about the importance of remaining optimistic even in the face of such large challenges.

What strikes me as most significant is that Browne is on the board of Intel, whose chair Dr. Gordon Moore has given billions of dollars to scientific research, conservation, and higher education. He also serves on the board of Goldman Sachs, one of the world's most prestigious investment banks, and under the leadership of Hank Paulson probably the most environmentally conscious.

The conversation has changed.

EACH OF US
STILL HAS TIME

Great contributions can be made late in one's career, regardless of what came before.

I often draw inspiration from the life of Abraham Lincoln, whose eventual success, both personal and societal, would have been hard to predict given his many business failures and electoral defeats. Like many of us today, he also had what now would be labeled depression, for him long periods of seriously questioning whether he could even go on.

Lincoln wrote his first extended statement on slavery 20 years before he became president. Yet, as Joshua Wolf Shenk writes, "at the time, Lincoln articulated no political point of view. His mind was elsewhere, trying to construct, from the throes of difficulty and uncertainty, a way of understanding ... who he was, where he was going in the world, and, indeed, whether he could survive."

"Yet this self-centered concern with his own suffering led him, slowly, to see and grapple with the suffering around him."

Lincoln had to find something great enough to live for.

Looking back from the very different world in which we live, can we imagine just how "out there," how utterly inconceivable, the end of slavery was? If that utopian, foolhardy, and naive aspiration was in fact possible, dare I ask what might be achievable today if not dismissed out of hand? Perhaps even the abolition of war? (Did I actually say that out loud?)

Today, individuals have more time to dedicate themselves to such honorable ambitions. You probably know that you're likely to live much longer than your great-grandparents did. Indeed, during the past century, life expectancy in the developed world has increased by 30 years. In effect, we've received the gift of an additional adult lifetime. I've known that for quite a while now and I'm still trying to fathom it.

All around us, people who focused the first half of their adulthood tending to business and family commitments are using the second half to invest themselves in society. A decade ago, I remember hearing that Bill Gates thought the jobs Microsoft created and the economic benefits of software development were sufficient contribution to the world. Agreed, that has been a contribution of historic proportion. Now, as this chapter was being written, the 50-year-old Gates announced he'd do even more and would be turning his main attention from Microsoft to his charitable foundation. Soon after, his friend Warren Buffet, some 25 years his senior, entrusted Gates' foundation with the largest philanthropic investment in history.

For you and me, as our lives become longer, a second calling becomes increasingly possible, indeed desirable—for both self and society.

Those who've taken on such roles (whether before retiring or after) have told us, in countless interviews, that their work in the social sector and civic arena has been even more important to them than the careers and businesses they spent decades building.

That may come as little surprise. After all, our investments in society may be the most significant expressions of who we are, what we stand for, and our hopes for the future. Through those commitments, we connect ourselves to humanity. We connect our generation with those yet to come.

Russell Simmons, the hip-hop producer we met earlier, says he'd rather be remembered as a philanthropist. "When I die, I hope they put that on my tombstone."

MEANING
AND IMMORTALITY

The desire to make a difference—the abiding search for meaning—grows with each passing decade, hand-in-hand with matters of the spirit and with our awareness that one day our physical presence on this Earth will come to an end. Our lives are longer, yet still finite.

Ernest Becker writes in *The Denial of Death*: "The only worthwhile preoccupation of man: What is one's true talent, his secret gift, his authentic vocation? What does a person dedicate him or herself to beyond the purely personal?"

Fidelity to such a life-affirming sense of purpose, beyond (and yet including) the self, is often referred to as a calling. In the Judeo-Christian use of the term, God calls the faithful to service. The Buddhist and Islamic notion of right livelihood holds a similar meaning for many. In a secular context, we might say that it is society that calls one to serve.

Our quest to locate and pursue that life-giving force is the most honest and brave way of facing our greatest anxiety, albeit one that's usually hidden even from ourselves: our own mortality. This search for purpose becomes even more important when we realize that the immortality motive may be the greatest human drive, as we strive to have tangible proof that *who we are* can outlive our bodily existence.

Creating the future, especially when it's wrapped up with our own mortality, seems like a pretty tall order.

Little wonder so many of us back away (and all of us back away at times) at future's door. We've said that our desire to create the world we want is often held back by our desire to be "realistic," to protect ourselves from disappointment, to avoid looking like a fool. It's only reasonable to tell ourselves the soothing story that what we want is just plain not possible, and besides, even if it were, we wouldn't deserve it and we couldn't make enough of a difference to matter.

Even the most courageous among us have these moments of doubt, as one of the heroes in this book wrote me after reading a draft of the manuscript. Rosemary Cairns, who shared her story of a meeting in northern Canada (and who is now working in a village in Serbia), said in her note, "Somehow I started to grieve about how powerful those default settings are—those messages in my childhood that say, 'You're getting above yourself' (what they used to say in Ireland, often). Somehow, I silence my own voice.

"There is a part of me that believes strongly in myself, and there is another part that is very uncertain."

Thank you, Rosemary, for saying it for me, and perhaps for others.

But as Steve Jobs put it so poignantly when he spoke to the 2005 graduating class at Stanford University, "Almost everything—all external expectations, all pride, all fear of embarrassment or failure—these things just fall away in the face of death, leaving only what is truly important. … There is no reason not to follow your heart."

When you and I attend to all that we have going for us (often right in front of us yet unseen, like an underground stream), we become aware that our choices are greater than we imagined. And we are emboldened to reach for those that matter most.

It is possible, although unusual, to talk about such aspirations in our public lives: in organizations of the social sector, in civic life, in the workplace. We can make space for conversations of consequence. We can talk about why we serve, why we give. We can allow what is most important to us, what we want our lives to be about and to have been about, to inform and strengthen our presence.

And whenever we do, we legitimize the pursuit of purpose and meaning, for ourselves and for others.

Once we acknowledge both the prospect of our own death and the promise that life holds, we gain our greatest power: the ability to use our lives to say something important, however small or large we may think it is. Our actions, our contributions, or just showing up in our own way, can send a message that means something to others, and even to ourselves.

If we make that choice for life, our civilization may not only be rescued from the worst of fates, we may be opened into the best of fates, beyond our imagination of today.

And along the way, you and I will come to know that we counted for something. That we mattered. That we were indeed alive.

What kind of world do you want to leave behind?

ACKNOWLEDGMENTS

I'm sitting aboard a Boeing 727 ready for take-off, thinking about what I might say to you in this section. I look out the window in awe at the incredible that has become the ordinary: This flight is a miracle of human organizing. I watch the synchronization of crew, catering, baggage, and what must be millions of complex elements, all coming together so that this 100-ton plane will ascend to the heavens in a few minutes. It's hard to know which is a greater triumph of the human spirit—the feat of organizing or the ingenuity of flight.

This book lives in an updraft of many people, too.

People like David Cooperrider, who permeates this book and my life. This book is possible only because of him, Fred Bleeke, John Carter, Gordon Johnson, Jane Watkins, and Diana Whitney.

I first heard the clarion call of global hope from Robert Muller, former assistant secretary general of the UN, in a series of meetings we had together at the UN University for Peace in Costa Rica ... a call echoed by Michael Bleks in his brave co-founding of Witten/Herdecke University, the first private university in Germany ... and sustained by Peter Seligmann's innovative mind and Charles Gibbs' brilliance and tenacity in the birthing of the United Religions Initiative.

I find it interesting that only after the writing was finished did I realize that most of those who contributed insightful and moving experiences are people who have participated in at least two workshops: Theresa Bertram, Dick Boysen, Dan Loritz, Debbie MacDougall,

Elinor Magnuson, and Ann Nickerson. And having been a member of four workshop cohorts was the woman you met in the last pages, Virginia Henderson, co-founder of the Australian national Shakespeare company and a long-time executive of the National Gallery of Australia. Cummings Zuill deserves special note for his role in the debut of the book.

Long-time friends, beginning with my buddy since we were four, Al Merkrebs, and Dave Huey, Warren Grossman, Joyce Hinckley, Carol Intihar, Lorraine Murphey, Bill VanBuskirk, and Eric Weir. And my family, the ground from which I grow.

The incubator for the ideas? The finest organizational behavior program in the world at the Weatherhead School of Management of Case Western Reserve University, and the experiential learning of the Gestalt Institute of Cleveland.

Thank you, Mrs. Elfrida Chappel (always affirming, "Good Lizzy," without a single correction for her Corgi), who lent me a cottage in Bermuda, and her hospitality.

All of you were in the room, the various rooms, where Pam and I thought, wrote, and rewrote this book.

When I told Pam I was ready to write this part, she said, "Remember your teacher who taught you to read and write." Of course, I'm still learning, thanks to Pam's ideas and values every bit as much as her writing and teaching abilities, all in one amazing person.

ABOUT
JIM LORD AND
PAM McALLISTER

JIM LORD's life has been dedicated to advancing society, beginning with a 1975 series of articles on quality of life in American cities. In the first decades of his work, he facilitated the investments that people wanted to make in social sector organizations. And indeed billions of dollars have been contributed to causes where Jim has served as "thinking partner," while one of his books for civic leaders remains the international all-time best-selling book in the field more than 20 years after its release.

Looking beyond the rewards of that pathway, he committed himself to expanding the idea of what could be possible for humanity, studying that question in intensive workshops with small groups of selected leaders from more than 50 countries. From that pioneering work, new ideas and practices emerged to advance society to its next level through causes and organizations of social good.

Now, more than a decade after the first learning lab, those discoveries have become available in *What Kind of World Do You Want?*

After nearly seven years in the private practice of corporate law, PAM McALLISTER left her firm the day before she was to have become a partner. She chose instead to make her contribution to society through environmental causes. Pam has been serving social sector organizations for more than 20 years in roles as diverse as volunteer, trustee, staff member, and communications advisor. She began her collaboration with Jim more than four years ago, when she began seeking new ideas that could bring renewed energy to the environmental movement—by changing the discourse surrounding the relationship between people and the rest of the natural world.

Notes

Notes

Notes

Notes

Notes